THE UNMASKING EFFECT

Awaken, Unmask, and Realign –
Your Path to Wholeness
& Inner Mastery

Ike Anderson

The Unmasking Effect: Awaken, Unmask, and Realign – Your Path to Wholeness & Inner Mastery

Print ISBN: 979-8-9903367-6-6

Publisher: **Author Writer's Academy**

AWA Literary Agency, United States

Senior Editor: Marjah Simon

www.AWA4Life.com

Cover Design and Illustrations – Author Writer's Academy

WELCOME TO
THE UNMASKING EFFECT

This is not just another book that will sit on your shelf. It's not a memoir, a self-help guide, or a timeless masterpiece. This book is about *you* – your awakening, your transformation, and your path to unmask your highest, most authentic self.

My ONE central transformation promise to you:

You now hold the seed to plant, nurture, and grow into a fully integrated, aligned life. This Blueprint will enable you to create happiness and balance in a purposeful way.

While I share insights from my own path, this book is designed to ignite something within you – a deeper awareness, a shedding of illusions, and a path toward living in full alignment. Ancient wisdom traditions have been a lifelong passion of mine, but wisdom is nothing without action. My hope is that this book serves as a gateway – an invitation to experience yourself on a more profound level.

As you begin this journey, I want to share a few tips and strategies for getting the most out of *The Unmasking Effect.*

Though this book unfolds sequentially, no single mask matters more than another. The flow ensures you examine different aspects of yourself at the right moment. If one resonates more deeply, that's perfect – it's exactly what should happen. This journey is uniquely yours.

Everyone is unique; everyone has their own personal blueprint. However, despite our uniqueness, the laws and processes that govern how we flow within our blueprints are the same for everyone.

This book aims to provide you with some methods of navigating your way through the blueprint.

I think it's important, therefore, to enter *The Unmasking Effect*, looking at everything from a new clear perspective. Think of it in terms of the idea of the "glass, half-empty" perspective. This is when you acknowledge that you don't know everything and you're not judging anything; you are just becoming aware of the existence of something that could bring fantastic meaning.

Beyond this:

- **Read With An Open Heart:** Embody the lessons, not just intellectually but in your daily life.

- **Immerse Yourself Fully:** Read slowly, reflect deeply, and allow insights to unfold naturally; see what resonates, what challenges you, and what sparks a shift.

- **Journal Your Journey:** Use prompts and reflections throughout the book to document your thoughts, breakthroughs, and evolving awareness. At the end of each Part, you'll find five powerful integration prompts. These questions are designed to turn your journal into your personal liberation blueprint – so this book doesn't just inspire you, it rebuilds you.

- **Honor Your Timing:** Unmasking isn't linear. Some realizations arrive instantly, while others take time. Trust your process.

- **Revisit as Needed:** Each chapter will reveal new insights depending on where you are in your journey. Return whenever you need clarity or guidance.

- **Explore More:** Additional resources are listed at the end of this book to support your continued journey.

Above all, as you read, I want you to keep asking yourself the following guiding question:

Who do I need to become to live
the most extraordinary life I can?

This book is more than words on a page – it's a guide to shedding the layers that have shaped your identity, healing the wounds of your past, and stepping into the wholeness of who you truly are. It unfolds step by step, yet it can also serve as a resource to revisit as you continue your journey of self-discovery

WHAT'S INSIDE
THE UNMASKING EFFECT

Part I: The Divine Purpose

Discover the foundation of what masks are, how they form, and what it takes to remove them. Explore how experiences, conditioning, and ancestral influences have shaped your sense of self, then begin aligning with your soul's essence.

Part II: Unmasking the Inner Child

Our earliest experiences leave deep imprints on our psyche. Delve into childhood conditioning, attachment wounds, and the protective masks we develop. Through guided reflections, you'll reconnect with your inner child – allowing space for healing, playfulness, and self-acceptance.

Part III: Unmasking Your Ancestry

Many of the burdens we carry are not solely our own. Explore generational trauma, inherited beliefs, and ancestral conditioning. By unearthing these influences, you'll gain insight into how history has shaped you – and learn how to honor your lineage while releasing what no longer serves you.

Part IV: Unmasking Societal Influences

Society imposes expectations that we unconsciously adopt. Examine cultural and systemic forces that encourage conformity and disconnect us from our true selves. By challenging these influences, you'll reclaim your own definitions of purpose, success, and fulfillment.

Part V: Unmasking the Cosmic Connection

Beyond personal and societal realms, there is a greater force at play – one that connects you to the universe. This section explores your spiritual essence, the interconnectedness of all things, and how aligning with cosmic forces can bring clarity, expansion, and belonging.

Part VI: Unmasking Wholeness

This final section weaves everything together, guiding you toward a life of integration and authenticity. Wholeness is not a final destination – it is an evolving process of deepening self-awareness and inner harmony.

Your Journey

Your unmasking journey is uniquely yours. This book serves as a guide, but the real transformation happens through your willingness to explore, question, and step fully into your power.

Take a deep breath, *surrender to the process*, and let's begin.

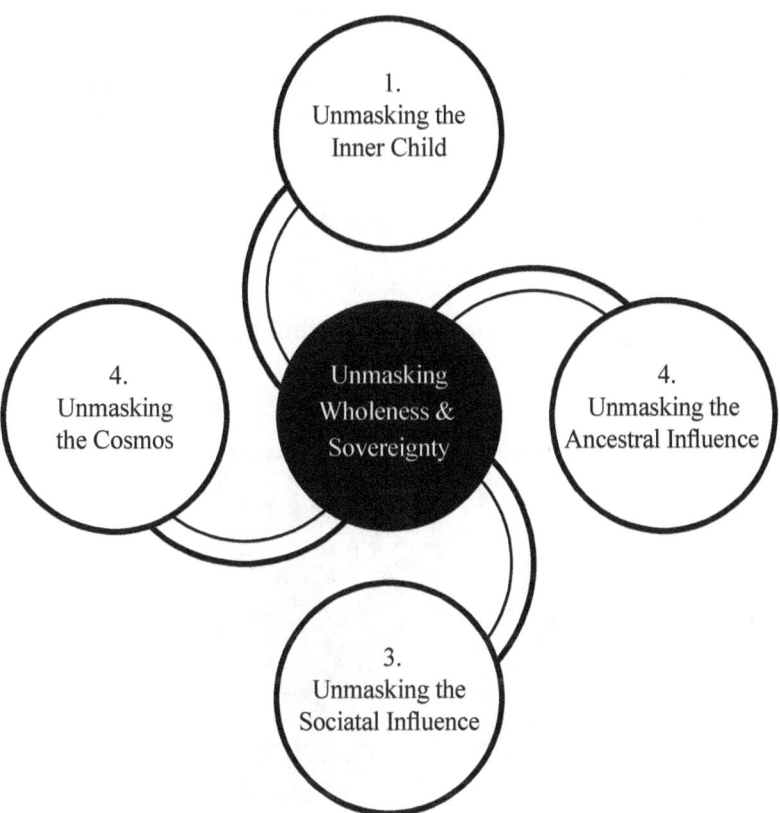

For Your Complimentary Resources

To support your journey with this book, download the
Unmasking Effect Worksheets – designed to accompany
and deepen your experience.

Visit: www.UnmaskingResources.com

These tools are here to help you reflect, integrate,
and embody the wisdom within these pages.

DEDICATION

To you … Yes, *you*...
The one who walks with questions deeper than words,
Who has heard the silent call echoing beyond the veil of ordinary life.

To the rememberers, the silent healers,
The edge-dwellers and light-bearers,
Who speak the language of stars and soil,
Who have died many small deaths
Only to rise wiser, softer, more whole,
This offering is for you.

This book is a temple of remembrance.
A key wrapped in ink.
A mirror for the unveiling.
A sacred companion on your return to what has always been.

Let these words stir what sleeps beneath your name.
Let them initiate you, not into something new,
But into the radiance you forgot you carried.

May each word unlock the sacred within you.
May you find, not just answers, but the echoes of your own knowing.
May your remembering awaken others.
May your light disrupt the slumber of fear.
And may you walk forward, not as a seeker, but as the flame itself.

ACKNOWLEDGEMENT

To my grandmother, Mamma, Evelyn Tracey Anderson

There are no words vast enough, no pages long enough, to fully capture the love and gratitude I hold for you. You were my rock, my guiding light, my safe place when the world felt too heavy to bear. When I lost my mother at just three years old, you stepped in – not just as a caregiver, but as my protector, my mentor, my greatest teacher. You gave me love so deep and unwavering that I never felt alone, even in my hardest moments.

You were there through every heartbreak, every failure, and every triumph. When I doubted myself, I only had to look into your eyes to see the belief you had in me – and that was enough to keep me going. When I stumbled in business, you reminded me that setbacks were stepping stones. When I won, you were my loudest cheerleader, celebrating my success as if it were your own.

I still hear your voice, Mamma, pushing me forward, challenging me to think beyond limits – reminding me that there is no box. I remember the way you made me read books, even when I resisted. You didn't just make me read; you made me reflect, discuss, and apply what I learned. You cultivated in me a love for wisdom, for curiosity, for thinking beyond the ordinary. That foundation shaped the man I am today, and without it, without you, this book would not exist.

Even though you are no longer here in body, I feel you in spirit – your love woven into every lesson, every word, every moment of this journey. I miss you beyond measure, but I carry you with me always.

This book is for you, Mamma. For your sacrifices, your wisdom, your love. For the unshakable faith you had in me, even before I could see it in myself. I love you. I honor you. I thank you.

– Always your grandson, with love beyond words.

To my wife, Natalee

From the very beginning, you have been by my side – through every dream, every risk, every late-night brainstorming session when all I had were ideas and an unshakable belief that somehow, someway, we would make it.

We started this journey when I was just 16, and for the past 28 years, you've been more than my partner – you've been my ride-or-die, my anchor, my greatest supporter. Through every high and low, you have been there, standing firm, holding me up when I was ready to fall, reminding me of my purpose when doubt crept in. When I wanted to quit, you saw the vision even when I couldn't, pushing me forward with your unwavering faith in me.

You have given me something priceless – unconditional safety and stability, a place to land no matter how high I soar or how hard I fall. Your love, patience, and belief in me have been the foundation beneath every step I've taken.

I could not have done this without you, and I would never want to. This book, this journey, and all that I am would not be the same without you in it. Thank you for being my partner in every sense of the word. I love you always.

To my children, Jasmine, Kaylee, and Layton

Jasmine, my firstborn, my wake-up call, my reason to see the world differently. You shifted everything for me, making me realize that I had to step up, not just for myself but for you. In moments when I felt like giving up, you were my motivation, my anchor, the reason I kept pushing forward. Your unconditional love has taught me patience, trust, and the beauty of simply being present. When you came into my life, I was filled with doubts – was I capable of being the father you deserved? But you showed me that love and presence mattered more than perfection. You made fatherhood not just possible, but a joy. I am endlessly grateful for you.

Kaylee, my daughter, my universe twin, born on the very same day as me. You reflect both my light and my shadows, mirroring parts of me in ways no one else does. Your challenges, your questions, your fearless demand for more from me – these push me to grow, to expand, to be better. You remind me daily that love is infinite and that there is always room to open my heart even wider. You've shown me depths of love I never thought possible, and for that, I am forever thankful.

Layton, my son, my protector. Your kindness, compassion, and unwavering sense of grace inspire me in ways I can't fully put into words. You forgive easily, love unconditionally, and always remind me of the power of a pure heart. You challenge me to embrace creativity over logic and to see the world through imagination and intuition rather than just structure and reason. Even at your young age, you carry the spirit of a guardian, always looking out for those you love, including me. And I know that no matter how many years pass – even when I'm 90 years old – you've got me, just as I've always got you.

Jasmine, Kaylee, Layton – you are my greatest teachers, my greatest inspirations, my greatest motivators. Everything I do, I do with you in mind. For all that you have given me, I am endlessly grateful.

To My Mother, Peggie

Mom, I love you beyond words. Though our time together was far too short, I know you brought me into this world for a reason before you had to go. You gave me the greatest gift – life itself – my very existence, your miracle baby. And for that, I am forever grateful.

Thank you for all that you sacrificed to bring me into this world. I often wonder what it would have been like to have you here, to hear your voice, to feel your embrace, to share life's moments with you. I miss you more than I can ever express, but I know your spirit has never truly left me. You walk with me, guide me, and protect me as one of my angels.

I wish you were here, but I carry you in my heart always. With this book, this journey, this life, I hope I am making you proud.

To My Dad, Dwight

Dad, I love you. I see you. I honor the journey you've walked – the weight you carried from such a young age when life demanded you become the man of your family at just 12 years old. Losing your father so early forced you to grow up fast and navigate challenges that no child should have to face, and yet, you persevered.

I acknowledge all that you've moved through, the struggles you've endured, and the resilience you've shown. Through it all, you remained kind, and that kindness did not go unnoticed. You've taught me so much, but most of all, you've shown me the importance of showing up – for family, for my kids, and for the ones who matter most.

Thank you for the support you've given me over the years. For every moment you stood by me, for every lesson – spoken and unspoken – I am grateful. Your journey has shaped mine, and I carry your strength with me always.

To My Mother-in-Law and Father-in-Law, Gretel and Bally

From the very beginning, you have embraced me with open arms, offering not just support but a deep sense of family and belonging. The love, generosity, and unwavering encouragement you have given me and my family mean more than words can express.

Whenever we needed anything – big or small – you gave without hesitation, never asking for anything in return. Your kindness has been a foundation for us, and your belief in me has been a silent force, pushing me forward even when doubt crept in.

Thank you for always standing by my side, for seeing my vision, and for supporting me in everything I set out to do. I hope this book makes you proud because you have been part of the journey, and I am endlessly grateful for you both.

To my friends, my extended family, my circle of unwavering support – you have been my anchors, my mirrors, and my challengers in the best way possible. Writing *The Unmasking Effect* was not a solitary journey; it was a shared experience, one made richer by the encouragement, accountability, and wisdom you poured into me.

Jahmar, Stephen, Phil, Orville, Terrence, and Javatis – thank you for holding me to the fire, for checking in, for making sure I stayed true to the process when I wanted to drift away. Your belief in me, in this book, and in the message I wanted to share made all the difference.

Mutica DeGregory Johnson, Gita Petkevica, Angel Fernandez, Lisa Henson, and Uncle Martin Anderson – each of you, in your unique way, has been a source of motivation, wisdom, and support when I needed it most. I honor and appreciate you more than I can say.

Arthur Magoulianiti, Thank you! – Arthur, you are the best big brother and best friend I could ever ask for. Your guidance and unwavering support have been nothing short of a gift.

To my teachers and guides – **Tony Robbins**, for years of mentorship and lessons that shaped my perspective; **Kojo Bentil, Lily Lambert, Monica Vasquez, Taita Hector, Prof. Rick Riccardi, Emyr Bussade** – each of you has played a role in guiding me deeper into my own unfolding, revealing truths that have helped shape this work.

To **Paul Baum, Art Blanchford, Bob Hurd** – Every conversation, every challenge, every moment of grace became part of the soil in which I rooted deeper into who I truly am. Thank you for being part of my unfolding.

To my **ancestors,** those who came before and those who will come after–you are woven into the fabric of this book, into the very essence of my being. Your presence is felt, your guidance is honored, and your legacy continues.

This book would not be what it is without each of you. Your words, your love, your lessons – both spoken and unspoken – have shaped this work in ways beyond what I can express. Thank you for seeing me, for walking with me, and for believing in what I had to say.

I am forever grateful.

SPECIAL THANKS

As far as we can discern,
the sole purpose of human existence
is to kindle a light in the darkness of mere being.
– Carl Jung

This book would not exist without the wisdom of Carl Jung. His teachings on the shadow, the psyche, and the wholeness of being laid the foundation for this work. Jung reminded us that wholeness isn't perfection-it's integration.

The Unmasking Effect is born from that same truth: that the masks we wear shape us, yet our ultimate purpose is to shed illusion and return to our authentic, true selves. Jung's exploration of the shadow, the collective unconscious, and individuation laid the foundation for this journey of unmasking – not to discard parts of ourselves, but to embrace them fully. His work reminds us that beyond every mask is the light of self-awareness, waiting to be remembered. This book is rooted on and builds on Jung's humanistic tradition.

CONTENTS

CONTENTS

CONTENTS

CONTENTS

INTRODUCTION

For years, I lived a life shaped by what others expected of me. Society had its vision for who I should be, my family had their hopes for what I should become, and somewhere along the way, I lost sight of myself. On the surface, I had it all: the career, the home, the checklist of achievements that signaled success. But inside, I felt hollow, like something fundamental was missing.

I never could work out what that something was, and I didn't realize how much I was racing through life until my 33rd birthday. That number held a deep significance because it was the age at which my mother passed away from cancer. Her death left an imprint; for the longest time, I believed that I, too, might be living on borrowed time. Subconsciously, I lived against an invisible clock, pursuing everything society claimed mattered: education, career, family, house, car. I thought if I could achieve it all before 33, I might finally feel complete.

But when the day came and went, I was still here – and I continue to be here. I had been given extra time, and I was determined to make it count.

Reflecting on my life, I saw how disconnected I had become from my true self. Deep inside, I was a free spirit. I wanted to live on the edges of life, to explore, to question, and to break free from the status quo. But the life I was leading – the life I had built – didn't reflect that.

The awakening came unexpectedly. During a parent-student lunch at my daughter's school, I watched as children – including my own daughter – filed into the cafeteria in perfect, silent lines.

Fingers pressed to lips, moving like tiny robots. Their individuality erased, their energy subdued. My chest tightened as discomfort washed over me.

What was I doing to my kids?
What was I doing to myself?

That night, I told my wife we needed to let go of everything – our house, our cars, the possessions we'd worked so hard to accumulate – and seek something greater. To my surprise, she didn't hesitate. She felt it, too.

Eight months later, we sold and donated nearly all our belongings. We decided to homeschool our children and embark on a journey guided by ancestral roots. Using DNA tests, we mapped out a path that would take us to the lands of our forebears. What began as a leap into the unknown turned into a six-year odyssey spanning over 100 countries.

The journey was far more profound than we could have imagined. Not only did we see the world, but all of us began the process of unmasking and stripping away the layers of conditioning, trauma, and societal expectations that had defined us for too long.

That process of unmasking took me through four key layers of healing:

- I unmasked my inner child, healing wounds I had carried since childhood.

- I unmasked ancestral patterns, releasing cycles of pain passed down through generations.

- I unmasked the weight of societal conditioning, freeing myself from expectations that didn't align with my truth.

- I unmasked the cosmic elements, awakening to the interconnectedness of all things and my role within the grand design.

Each layer brought its own challenges, but together, they led me toward wholeness.

Wholeness isn't about perfection; it's about integration. It means recognizing that every part of who you are has value: your light and shadow, your strengths and weaknesses. It's weaving those parts together into a cohesive whole, where nothing is rejected or suppressed.

Sovereignty and wholeness are deeply intertwined. Sovereignty is the ability to live authentically, in alignment with your truth; it reveals how we find and embody our purpose. But you can't claim sovereignty without first achieving wholeness. And wholeness isn't a destination you reach once; it's a way of being. It's an ongoing journey of self-discovery, growth, and alignment.

As children, we are full of questions. We are curious about every aspect of the world, and we want to know everything, from questions with the simplest of answers to questions that philosophers have been asking for millennia:

Why are we here?
What is the meaning of life?
What lies beyond what we can see?

These were questions that followed me into adulthood, but I didn't realize how deeply they shaped me until I began this journey. Slowly, I was able to uncover the answers, but it wasn't in a single moment of clarity or life-changing epiphany, but in layers, as I removed one mask after another and moved through each phase of healing.

Each mask we wear serves a purpose at some point in our lives.

As children, we develop masks to protect ourselves from pain, to fit in, to meet expectations, to survive, and even to succeed. But as adults, those same masks can become barriers, keeping us from living authentically.

However, while the process is not easy, we can begin to remove our masks and reconnect with our true selves. It's a process that will take time and has many layers, but it opens the way to a life of purpose, bliss, and freedom.

When I began unmasking my inner child, I had to confront memories and emotions I had buried for decades; losing my mother at the age of three left a scar I hadn't fully acknowledged. My ancestral unmasking while standing in the slave dungeons of Ghana allowed me to face the weight of generational trauma but also recognize the resilience and strength of my ancestors. I realized that much of what I carried wasn't mine alone; it was a legacy passed down through the bloodline and generations.

Societal unmasking surprised me the most. I had built a life that looked good on paper but wasn't aligned with my authentic self. Society's expectations about success, masculinity, and parenting had shaped my choices in ways I hadn't even been aware of. Letting go of those expectations was like shedding a heavy cloak I didn't know I was wearing.

Finally, cosmic unmasking brought it all together. It's one thing to heal the wounds of the past; it's another to awaken to the infinite possibilities of the present. As I connected with cosmic energies, spirit guides, and universal truths, I began to see my place in the grand design. I understood that we're all part of something much larger than ourselves, and that realization brought a sense of peace and purpose I had never known or experienced.

Unmasking allowed me to release myself – my past, present, and future – from cycles and patterns that no longer served me or those around me. Through this process, I came to understand that wholeness isn't just a personal journey; it's a way of **BEING** that radiates outward. It's about living authentically, where your inner world and outer expressions are in harmony.

The Unmasking Effect does not prescribe a path. It shares what I've learned in the hopes of inspiring you to begin your own journey. This is your call to awaken, unmask, and realign.

Will you accept it?

Will you step beyond the limitations of what you think you know and uncover the truth of who you are?

The path is waiting.

So let's begin.

PART I
THE DIVINE PURPOSE

"There is the ultimate purpose,
which is to remember,
and in remembering, you remind others."
– Ike Anderson

CHAPTER 1

THE MASK

What You Will Unmask

In this chapter, I begin to see the masks I've worn my whole life – masks I didn't even know were there. And as I uncover them, I invite you to do the same. If you've ever felt like you're performing, hiding, or shape-shifting to belong... this chapter is your mirror. You'll start to recognize the ways you've protected yourself just to feel safe. And in doing so, you'll begin reclaiming the version of you that doesn't need to perform to be worthy.

To truly understand the concept of the mask, we must first acknowledge that it's not a single thing – it's a collection of personas and projections we present to the world. The mask is any version of ourselves that we offer to others, not necessarily based on who we truly are but on what we feel is expected, accepted, or safe.

At its core, the mask is a representation of ourselves that comes into being through various influences. We begin with our authentic self – the person we were born to be, pure and untainted by the world. Then, as we grow, we accumulate external influences: our parents, society, and experiences that shape our beliefs, actions, and identity.

The mask, in this sense, is more than just a shield – it is both protection and projection. It's a carefully crafted illusion shaped by our longing for acceptance and belonging. We wear it to fit in, to be loved, to meet the expectations imposed upon us. At first, it feels like a choice, a tool to navigate the world. But over time, it becomes more than a facade – we grow attached to it, and in that attachment, we blur the lines between who we are and who we pretend to be.

Yet we aren't the only ones who believe in this mask. Through the power of projection, others come to accept it as our truth as well. The world reflects the version of ourselves we present, reinforcing the illusion until it feels inescapable. The danger lies in forgetting that the mask was never our essence – it was merely a role we learned to play. To remove it is to risk rejection, to stand vulnerable in the rawness of authenticity. But only by unmasking can we reclaim the truth of who we are, beyond the projections and performances, and step into the full expression of our being.

But here's the truth: **the mask is never who we truly are**.

Over time, these layers build up, becoming thicker, more rigid, and calcified. They hide our natural self beneath, creating a version that feels authentic but is actually inauthentic. When we live behind these layers without questioning them, we risk losing sight of who we are meant to be.

This journey of self-discovery is about peeling back those layers and uncovering the person we are beneath all the fear, anxiety, and conditioning. It's about reconnecting with our true selves, free from the influences that have shaped us and the expectations that no longer serve us.

This realization came when I saw that the life I was living wasn't the life I truly wanted. It was a life shaped by others – by my parents' desires, by the need to fit in, and by societal expectations. I wanted to be admired and respected, but these desires weren't truly for me.

I pursued them to craft an image, to shield myself from judgment and rejection. It wasn't about genuine fulfillment but about appearing worthy in others' eyes. I craved acceptance and wanted to be seen as hardworking, even when I wasn't fully living up to it.

But living for others, living to prove something to someone else, is living behind a mask. It's a life of inauthenticity, where we constantly try to meet external standards at the cost of our own internal truth. When we focus too much on what others might think of us, we lose sight of who we truly are. The mask becomes our reality, and that's when we start to disconnect from our ultimate purpose.

The masks we've worn for so long no longer serve us. It's time to find the courage to **unmask** and live authentically.

OUR AUTHENTIC SELVES

The natural self is who we are at our core, before we were shaped by external influences and before we started wearing masks to protect ourselves or project a version of ourselves to the world. In our purest form, without the weight of those masks, we are aligned with our ultimate purpose: to remember, to remember who we truly are, to remember the wisdom that lies within, and in doing so, to help others remember as well.

When we shed the masks, we tap into a state of being healthier, more vibrant, and are more attuned to the energies around us. We begin living a beautiful life and contributing to the world in meaningful, genuine ways. Life becomes a process of continuous growth and healing. We feel the bliss of simply existing, deeply connected to the rhythm of the universe and open to the nudges that guide us along the way.

A heightened awareness comes with living in our natural state. Our senses become sharper: we hear more clearly, feel more deeply, and experience life with a greater presence. We're no longer distracted by the need for validation or approval. Instead, we begin to hear our true self, the one aligned with the bigger picture.

This shift impacts how we relate to others, too.

When you're not caught up in the need to impress or fit in, you form more genuine, meaningful relationships. Instead of small talk about trivial matters, you dive deeper and connect with people beyond the surface, sharing experiences and truths that bring you closer together.

This is the beauty of living as your natural self. Behind the mask, we try to live the perfect life, but there is no such thing as perfect.

Living as your natural self means living with true authenticity, embracing the journey, and moving through it with awareness and openness rather than avoiding challenges or fear. **When we live from this place, we not only grow ourselves but help others grow,** creating a ripple effect that deepens our connections with the world.

THE ACCUMULATION OF MASKS

From childhood, we develop masks shaped by our fears, often unconscious ones, that begin with seeking parental approval and validation. These early experiences teach us to become people-pleasers rather than boundary-setters, forming our first masks of trying to be "good enough."

As we mature, fears of judgment, failure, and rejection lead us to create more masks for different contexts – school, friends, and work. While masks help us adapt, they gradually obscure our authentic selves. Without awareness, these layers accumulate like thick makeup until we lose touch with who we truly are beneath them.

The discovery of our masks often starts when we notice moments of feeling inauthentic. Experiences like being excluded, feeling inadequate, and facing rejection may seem small but leave lasting impacts. In response, we create masks as armor against future pain. Yet, this protection doesn't heal our wounds; it merely conceals them. Eventually, we may become so skilled at wearing these masks that we mistake them for our true identity.

Unmasking isn't an intellectual exercise but a lived experience of peeling back these layers to rediscover our authentic selves. It requires confronting our core fears of being unloved, judged, or inadequate. The journey isn't about angrily tearing away these protective layers but learning to live authentically despite our fears. It's about recognizing moments of inauthenticity as opportunities for growth and gradually shedding false identities to live with greater clarity and connection.

THE MASKS
THAT SPAN GENERATIONS

Masks accumulate over time, layering over our authentic selves, and often persist long after we are gone. We inherit them from our ancestors, and we pass them on to our successors. If we keep doing the same things, we'll keep getting the same results. That's the essence of it. From generation to generation, different masks can be passed down under the guise of patterns and tradition. While some are worth preserving, like bringing strength, wisdom, and resilience, others are like flaws in a mold. They create imperfections in everything that follows.

Imagine baking a cake in a tin with a deep dent. No matter how perfect the recipe or how carefully you prepare the batter, the finished cake will always bear the mark of that dent. It's not the cake's fault, but the flaw gets passed along. This is what happens with unaddressed issues in our lineage.

Ancestral healing is like fixing that dented tin. It's about breaking the cycle so that future outcomes, whether in behavior, emotional patterns, or relationships, are no longer shaped by inherited burdens.

That is the essence of ancestral work. You may not have been the one who experienced the trauma, made the choices, or carried the belief, but you are the receiver of its impact. The weight of unexamined stories, habits, and fears gets handed down, generation after generation, until someone steps up to address it.

My grandmother had a saying: "The fathers have eaten sour grapes, and the children's teeth are set on edge." It speaks to how suffering trickles down through generations, how the mistakes of the past leave imprints on those who come after.

For centuries, people believed that they were trapped by the decisions of their ancestors, doomed to repeat the same struggles. But there's another side to this: we are not condemned to carry what doesn't serve us. Just as the prophets, Ezekiel and Jeremiah later challenged this belief, we, too, have the power to rewrite our stories.

The truth is, while we may inherit wounds, behaviors, and emotional burdens, we are also given the opportunity to change them. That is the difference between unconscious repetition and conscious transformation. Healing the ancestral line is a way of taking responsibility, not for what happened before us, but for what we choose to carry forward.

To unmask these elements, we must recognize what's been passed down and decide what to keep and what to change. It's about honoring the past without being trapped by it. When we do the work of healing ancestral patterns, we're not just freeing ourselves; we're creating a new legacy for those who come after us.

This process is both personal and collective. On a personal level, it involves looking inward, examining the beliefs and behaviors you've inherited, and asking: *Does this serve me? Does this align with who I want to be?* On a collective level, it's about acknowledging how these inherited patterns ripple out and shape the world we live in.

True unmasking is about taking the lessons from the past and consciously shaping a different future. It's about baking the cake in a new tin, free of dents, so the next generation can start with something whole.

What You Have Unmasked

*By the end of this chapter, I've begun the work of unmasking –
and so have you. Have you started to name your own disguises,
question your patterns, and feel the weight you've been
carrying? You've been given permission to let go of the version
of you that was built for survival – so you can begin becoming
the version that was born for truth.*

CHAPTER 2
UNMASKING THE TRUTH

What You Will Unmask

*In this chapter, I go deeper into the truth behind the masks –
not just why we wear them but what they're actually here to
teach us. If you've ever felt stuck in a version of yourself that
no longer fits, this chapter will help you shift from self-blame to
self-awareness. You'll begin to understand the purpose behind
your performance – how your masks were never mistakes but
messages. And by seeing the mask clearly, you get closer to
who you truly are underneath it all.*

The masks may feel like armor, but they're not. They don't truly
protect us; they only distance us from ourselves. At some point, we all
face the choice: Do we keep piling on the layers, or do we start
peeling them back?

For many, the process of unmasking begins with a moment of self-
awareness. This moment can be a life-changing event that forces us to
reevaluate everything, or it can be a quieter realization, a nagging
sense that we're not living authentically. Either way, it's a
confrontation with the truth. And truth, while liberating, is rarely easy.

It requires revisiting those early experiences of rejection, fear,
and inadequacy and seeing them for what they truly are.

This isn't about blaming others or ourselves; it's about acknowledging buried feelings and understanding how they've shaped us. If we avoid this work, those unresolved feelings continue to hold us back, dictating our actions and clouding our sense of self.

When confronted with our true selves, when we have that chance to look inward, some people push back and continue to live behind their masks, while others will choose to face themselves. It's not easy, but those who choose to rediscover and reconnect with their natural self take the first step toward living a truly incredible life – one of their own design.

Unmasking is not about perfection; it's about honesty. It's about choosing authenticity over illusion and truth over comfort.

There is a tale in Egyptian mythology that talks about what one experiences while traveling through the Duat, the Egyptian underworld. The first ritual the deceased must go through is the weighing of the heart. This ritual takes place in the Hall of Ma'at, the goddess of truth, harmony, and justice. Here, they were to own every part of themselves and recite every sin they had committed in life. Then, Anubis would weigh their hearts against the feather of Ma'at, a symbol of purity and balance. If the heart was as light as the feather, the individual was deemed worthy and moved forward. If it was heavy with unexamined burdens – regrets, dishonesty, unresolved pain – it was consumed by the Devourer of Souls, Ammit, a fearsome creature: part lion, part crocodile, part hippo.

For me, this symbolizes the universal truth that life demands balance. The heart represents the self, our essence, weighed down by the masks we wear and the truths we avoid. If we fail to confront the weight of these masks and choose to live in denial, there comes a point where those burdens must be reckoned with. While we might not be consumed by the Devourer of Souls, it might manifest as a sense of incompleteness in life or a missed opportunity for fulfillment.

The weighing of the heart also speaks to the liberation that comes from unmasking. When we remove the layers of fear, judgment, and rejection, and when we own every part of ourselves and live in our true selves, our hearts become lighter.

Whether you see this process as spiritual, symbolic, or simply psychological, the message is the same. We are meant to examine ourselves, to weigh the burdens we carry, and to let go of what no longer serves us. If we don't, the consequences aren't external punishment; they're the loss of the life we could have lived. But if we do, then the reward is a life of lightness, balance, and true alignment with who you are.

FROM SELF-AWARENESS TO COLLECTIVE AWAKENING

Unmasking starts as an individual journey. It's deeply personal as you confront your own layers, understand the intricacies of what shaped you, and uncover the hidden steps that lead to alignment. But the power of this process doesn't end with you. Once you have begun to take your masks off, the next step is to bring others into the fold, to guide and support those who are also seeking answers and connection.

For me, this means documenting the four frameworks I went through in my own unmasking journey. It's about distilling the knowledge, the hidden truths, and even the initiations I've encountered so others can navigate their paths with more clarity. This isn't about giving people a rigid formula, but offering tools and insights that allow them to find their unique truths.

Unmasking starts with self-awareness but expands to a collective awakening – it becomes a shared experience. When you've done the work on yourself, you're in a position to uplift others, creating a cycle of growth and contribution that strengthens not just individuals but entire communities.

THE ALCHEMY OF MASKS FOR TRANSFORMATION, NOT CONCEALMENT

After everything you've just read, what I am about to say may come across as contradictory. When you discover the existence of your masks, it's easy to think of them as something to be entirely discarded, leaving your pure, natural self. But the truth is more nuanced than that.

Sometimes, wearing a mask can be necessary.

As I've grown in self-awareness, I've come to understand that not all masks are harmful or inauthentic. Stepping into different roles, for example, often requires creating a new identity – a mask, in a sense.

I've had to learn how to embody the mask of Ike, the father, with all the responsibilities, love, and care that role demands. I've taken on the mask of Ike, the entrepreneur, navigating challenges and leading with purpose. I've even adopted the mask of Ike, the spiritual healer, stepping into a space of guidance and connection for others.

These aren't masks I wear to hide or deceive; they're masks I consciously choose that help me bring my authentic self into different areas of life. They're not about pretense but about integration. They allow me to take the lessons I've learned on my journey and channel them into roles that serve not just myself but others as well.

This is why I don't want to demonize masks or suggest we should burn them all in some symbolic flame. The key isn't to eliminate masks but to become aware of them. When we're conscious of the masks we wear, why we wear them, and how they serve us, we gain the ability to choose them intentionally and remove the ones that are no longer serving us or our truth.

In this way, masks can become tools for growth and connection. They allow us to integrate the truths we've uncovered into our daily lives. They help us navigate the complexities of relationships, responsibilities, and societal roles without losing sight of who we truly are beneath them.

It's about balance. The danger lies not in wearing a mask but in forgetting it's a mask. When we're unaware and allow the mask to define us, that's when we lose touch with our natural self. But when we approach life with awareness and intention, masks can actually become a means of expressing our authenticity in different contexts.

This process is about shedding the masks we've developed unconsciously and moving towards adopting masks that assist us purposefully.

So, the question isn't whether masks are good or bad; it's whether we're wearing them consciously. Are we choosing masks that align with our growth and values? Are we integrating the lessons of unmasking into the roles we play? Because when we do, masks can become powerful tools for helping ourselves and others rather than barriers to authenticity.

What You Have Unmasked

*I began to see my masks not as lies but as language –
parts of me trying to communicate my unmet needs.
And so did you. Where have you started to reclaim
compassion for your past selves, release judgment,
and embrace the possibility that even your protection
has been part of your path? This chapter reminded
both of us: unmasking isn't destruction; it's alchemy.
It's how you transform survival into sovereignty.*

CHAPTER 3

THE UNIVERSAL PURPOSE

What You Will Unmask

*In this chapter, I begin exploring the deeper truth of purpose –
not the one assigned to us by society or family, but the one
written into the core of my being. And as I step into this
exploration, I'm inviting you to do the same. You'll start to
sense the possibility that your life isn't random. That the pain,
the patterns, and the path all hold meaning. This chapter helps
you shift from searching for a purpose outside yourself to
uncovering the one you've carried all along. If you've ever
asked, "Why am I really here?"
this is where answers begin to rise.*

Across all cultures and traditions, humanity's pursuit of meaning has
led to a common thread, a search for universal truths. The names
and interpretations differ, but the essence remains the same: our
purpose is to remember who we are, and in that remembering, to
share it with the world.

This remembering is not a simple act of recalling who we are in this
life. It goes far deeper. It begins with the soul, the eternal essence that
animates us. The soul isn't bound to this body or this moment; it's
ancient, carrying the wisdom of countless lifetimes.

In India, it's called the Monad. In West Africa, it's the Ori, and in Ghana, the Kra. Each teaching holds that the soul incarnates to grow, evolve, and fulfill its divine journey. Take Buddhism, for instance. It speaks of Karma and Dharma – our past actions that we must resolve and the duties we must fulfill to align with our purpose. This process brings us closer to liberation, or Moksha.

Different cultures may have distinct words and frameworks, but they all point to the same truth: the soul's purpose is to expand, learn, and grow.

When we bring this understanding together, the bigger picture emerges. We're here to remember who we are, not just as individuals but as part of something greater. There's a micro and macro aspect – a connection between what is above and what is below. It's about integrating those perspectives, finding unity within duality, and embracing the wholeness of existence.

This is how we reconnect with the divine, the greater source and power that is truly infinite. We are not separate from it; we are simply a fragment of it, and on this journey, we realize that we and everyone and everything else are already a part of that interconnected oneness.

This "knowing" also calls us to action. It calls us to serve others, show kindness, and offer unconditional love. Each of us has a unique soul calling, and when we align with it, we discover ways to uplift those around us. How much love can we give? How deeply can we inspire others to rise? Those things, too, are central to our human journey.

But we must also recognize the union of body, mind, and spirit. The body is a sacred vessel – the human suit we are given to experience life. Taking care of it allows us to engage fully in the world, climb mountains, nurture others, and immerse ourselves in the contrasts of joy and pain, light and dark. The mind must be developed through wisdom, understanding, and integration, learning not just intellectually but in a way that is applied and embodied.

The spirit is nurtured by connecting with the higher essence of the elements, the divine, our ancestors, and the benevolent forces that support us.

Life is not isolating; it's a sacred cycle that binds growth, love, and unity into a single, universal truth. It's about remembering, reconnecting, and contributing. No matter where we come from, we are all seeking the same light. Yet, it is important to remember that the divine purpose has no final destination. Experiencing, learning, and growing is the journey. The places we explore, things we learn, and people we love create the meaning that centers our lives.

In the end, process is purpose, and purpose is process.

THE UNITY OF ONENESS

Unmasking isn't just about shedding personal layers; it's about revealing our connection to something greater. The masks we wear shape our individual identities and create the illusion that we are separate from each other. In truth, we are deeply interconnected and are privileged to be part of a shared human experience that stretches across generations.

The Hawaiian practice of Ho'oponopono speaks directly to this. It teaches that healing is not just a personal act but a collective responsibility. By acknowledging our role in the patterns we inherit and contribute to, we take accountability for our part in the larger whole. This philosophy mirrors the unmasking process: recognizing what we carry, releasing what no longer serves us, and stepping into a clearer, more authentic way of being.

Humanity, unlike other animals, exists in and is defined by its ability to experience contrast: joy and sorrow, light and dark, struggle and triumph. Many of the masks we wear are defenses against this reality, attempts to shield ourselves from pain or uncertainty. True unmasking requires integration, not avoidance. To heal, we must allow space for all aspects of our experience, understanding that pain and growth are not opposites but partners in transformation.

This process doesn't happen in isolation. The imprints we carry – whether ancestral, cultural, or societal – shape our thoughts, behaviors, and emotional patterns. Unmasking these layers is more than personal healing; it's a way of breaking generational cycles and shifting the collective consciousness.

During my travels in Ghana, India, Ireland, and Scotland, I felt this deeply. Each place carried its own ancestral weight, and being present with it unearthed aspects of myself I hadn't previously recognized.

I saw how history lingers in the land, in the stories passed down, and in the unconscious patterns still playing out. Acknowledging these imprints allowed me to heal personally and also contribute to something larger – the restoration of truth, connection, and wholeness.

Unmasking is an invitation to see beyond the individual self, to recognize that personal healing ripples outward. When we remove the illusions that keep us divided – whether within ourselves or from each other – we open the door to unity. We begin to embody both our human and divine nature, not as separate forces but as one.

THE BODY

The body is more than just a vessel; it's the first mask we wear, and it allows us to experience life in its fullest form. It's the interface between our inner world and the physical realm, shaping how we move, feel, and interact with everything around us. Yet, like any mask, it can be neglected, misunderstood, or worn improperly, limiting our ability to fully engage with life.

Taking care of the body means honoring it as the sacred vessel it is. It's not about perfection; it's about function. A neglected body dulls experience, restricts freedom, and makes even the simplest joys feel out of reach. When we ignore our physical well-being, we unconsciously place barriers between ourselves and the life we're meant to live. Maintaining health isn't just about longevity – it's about presence. It's about making sure that when life calls, you're able to answer.

"Take care of your body.
It's the only place you have to live."
– Jim Rohn

The truth of Jim Rohn's quote hit me in an unexpected way during my honeymoon with my wife, Natalee. One morning, as our cruise ship docked, I noticed an older man sitting quietly on the deck. Something about his presence made me want to sit with him.

He told me his story. He had spent his youth consumed by work, always pushing life's experiences to a future that never arrived. Now, in his later years, his body wouldn't allow him to do the things he had once dreamed of. He looked at me and said, *"Do what you can while you're young and able."* His words weren't just advice; they were a warning.

Our bodies won't always be as strong or capable as they are right now. Taking care of them isn't just about health; it's about keeping the door open to life itself. The stronger and more vibrant your body is, the more you can experience and the longer you can sustain those experiences. Start early, take care of yourself, and you'll be able to create a lifetime of memories.

That is what it means to unmask the body, not to see it as a burden, an afterthought, or something to be judged, but as the very foundation for living fully. The body is not separate from the mind or the spirit; it is the gateway that allows us to express, to feel, and to move through the world with intention. To neglect it is to limit your connection to the world and to yourself. Honor it, nurture it, and it will carry you through this sacred journey.

THE UNITY OF MIND AND SPIRIT

Taking care of the mind begins with wisdom, understanding, and integration.

Wisdom is about continuous learning and growth. If you're not learning or growing, you're stagnating – or worse, metaphorically dying. For me, learning is a constant process. Right now, I'm delving into human design, a system that merges ancient divination practices like the I Ching, astrology, numerology, and the Kabbalistic tree of life. It's a fascinating exploration of who I am, offering insight into my cosmic blueprint – my strengths, my shadows, and the patterns shaped by the time and place of my birth.

Through this learning, I expand my understanding of myself, and as I expand, I can help others on their own journeys. That's the beauty of growth, but learning alone isn't enough. **Understanding** comes from integrating what you've learned, turning information into lived experience. Many people say, "Oh yeah, that makes sense," but then never apply that learning in their own life. Without action, knowledge remains inert. True understanding comes when you implement what you've learned, make it your own, and allow it to shape your life.

Integration, however, also means knowing when to let go. At different stages in life, certain beliefs or tools serve us well, but they may lose relevance as we evolve. Take religion, for example. For many, it provides a foundation of love and support at one stage, but as they grow, they may realize that the strength they sought externally already exists within them. The key is to recognize when to release what no longer serves you, and embrace what propels you forward.

This process naturally connects to nurturing the spirit, which is about moving within ourselves and deepening our connection to something greater. The spirit is the bridge between the self and the divine.

It's about not seeking outside of ourselves but realizing that the divine spark we long for is already within us. The connection comes through awareness, reflection, and alignment with the higher forces that guide and support us.

On my journey, I've learned that everything is interconnected. As I've traveled, I've seen ancient sites – pyramids, temples, and sacred spaces – built with uncanny precision and aligned with the stars. No matter the continent or culture, these monuments are a sign that for as long as we have walked this earth, we have always looked to the cosmos for answers. This understanding is woven into divination systems like human design, which show us how to integrate cosmic awareness into our human experience.

Ultimately, caring for the mind and spirit brings wisdom into action, allowing the knowledge of who you are to transform how you show up in the world. It's about integrating growth, releasing what no longer serves, and aligning with the divine essence within you. This alignment allows us to move through life not just as individuals but as connected beings, part of something far greater than ourselves.

CONTENTMENT, TRUTH, OR BOTH?

In Utilitarianism, there's a saying, *"It is better to be a 'human being' dissatisfied than a pig satisfied; better to be Socrates dissatisfied than a fool satisfied."* It's a saying that forces us to consider two seemingly opposing paths – ignorant contentment or enlightened dissatisfaction. I've thought about this often, and it's one of those ideas that keeps revealing more the more I reflect on it.

The satisfied pig represents the person with their head in the sand, oblivious to the deeper truths of life but seemingly content. Everything is surface-level, "great" on the outside, with no thought given to what lies beneath. And I'll admit, part of me finds that enviable at times. There's a simplicity to it, a kind of shield from the weight of life's complexities – just like the masks we wear. But it's fascinating that so many people can go through life untouched by deeper questions, unaffected by the struggles that seem to consume others.

But is it really great … or is it just a facade?

That's the question that lingers.

Then there's the dissatisfied Socrates – the seeker of truth who can never fully rest because the answers always lead to more questions. While there's wisdom in this path, it can also feel relentless. You might uncover insights and revelations, but the journey itself can become exhausting if it's only about seeking and never about living.

Is it truly better to be a dissatisfied Socrates? Is it better to be a human being dissatisfied?

What I've come to realize is that life isn't about choosing between these two extremes. It's not about rejecting the simplicity of the pig or becoming consumed by the endless search of Socrates.

It's about integrating both. Both the satisfied pig and the dissatisfied Socrates are parts of us, and each has something to teach.

A satisfied fool reminds us to embrace the simple joys of life – the beauty of being present, the peace that comes from letting go of overthinking, and the value of gratitude for what is. Meanwhile, existing as a human being challenges us to grow, to ask questions, and to deepen our understanding of ourselves and the world around us. We can be satisfied and dissatisfied at the same time; we can be content with what we have and have a need to expand, grow, and reach new heights.

The key is balance.

But how do you take what you need from the pig *and* from Socrates? How do you honor both the light and the dark within yourself?

This is where integration comes in – moving past the need to choose one over the other and instead embracing the duality of life.

Life is not about having all the answers because that would defeat the purpose of asking questions. It's about living in the tension between simplicity and depth, between ignorance and wisdom, and finding harmony in the journey. That's where the true richness of life lies – not in choosing one path but in learning to walk both.

INTEGRATION AND AWARENESS: THE DANCE OF BECOMING

Integration is the bridge between experience and embodiment, the alchemy of turning lessons into lived wisdom. It wasn't just an abstract concept for me; it was the pulse of my journey, a rhythm in which I had to learn to move. Awareness came first – awareness of who I truly was beneath the layers of conditioning, beyond the expectations I once lived for.

At first, I thought awakening was about knowledge, about learning profound truths that would somehow change me. But awareness alone wasn't enough. I had to live it. That was the difference between *knowing the path* and *walking it*. Walking it meant stripping away the masks, the false identities I had built for protection, the personas I wore to be accepted.

Every human being carries a piece of the divine, a spark of something infinite. Different cultures have described this understanding in their own way: Karma and Dharma in Buddhism, the Ori in West African traditions, the cosmic symphony reflected in astrology. But they all point to the same truth: we are here to remember. We are to remember who we are beyond survival, beyond societal roles, beyond the projections we've absorbed.

But remembering is only the beginning. It is one thing to recognize your own rhythm; it is another to dance to it. At first, I hesitated. Would I still be accepted if I moved to my own beat? Would I be judged if I let go of the performance? But I knew something deeper was calling me. I had spent too long living *to be seen* rather than living to *be*. So, I let the rhythm take over.

I think back to the nights I spent in places where the drum dictated movement, where the fire flickered in sync with the heartbeat of the earth. In many cultures, especially in Africa, the drum is more than an instrument – it is a vibration, a force that reminds us of something primal and eternal. The dance that follows is not about perfection; it is about surrender. It is about losing yourself and, paradoxically, finding yourself in the process.

When we dance freely to the rhythm of life, others take notice. They do not notice because we are teaching or because we are demanding they follow but because our authenticity *resonates*. Like in those ancient fire dances, each person must find their own rhythm. They may hear yours and be inspired by it, but they cannot move to your beat. They must listen for their own.

Integration begins with healing, bringing to light the hidden wounds that dictate our choices, releasing what no longer aligns, and embracing what does. The more we shed, the more space we create – not just for ourselves but for those around us. When we show up as our true selves, we give silent permission for others to do the same. As we lift our own masks, we make it easier for others to remove theirs. This is how the individual journey becomes a collective one.

In the end, we are all dancing around the same fire, each moving to a beat that was always within us, waiting to be heard.

UNLEARNING!
THE SPACE BETWEEN
WHO I WAS AND WHO I COULD BE

For so long, I thought the journey of purpose was about gaining more knowledge, more wisdom, more insight. I believed that the more I learned, the more I would grow. What I didn't realize was that learning alone wasn't enough. Just as important – if not more – was the process of *unlearning*.

Unlearning is the peeling away of layers, the release of beliefs that once felt like truth but no longer fit the person we are becoming. It's the uncomfortable process of shedding identities that kept us safe but now keeps us small. I didn't understand that until life forced me into it.

My own unlearning came through what I now know was my "dark night of the soul." At the time, I didn't have a name for it. All I knew was that everything I had built my life around – my faith, my relationships, and my identity – felt like it was crumbling. The world I had created, the version of myself I had carefully constructed, suddenly didn't make sense anymore.

It was like standing in a burning house. I could either run, clinging to whatever I could carry, or I could let the fire consume it all, including me, and trust that something new would emerge from the ashes.

For a long time, I resisted. I tried to hold onto the old truths, the ones that once gave me comfort. But the harder I gripped them, the more they burned. The *why* questions haunted me. "Why am I here? What is my purpose? Who am I if I let go of everything I thought I was?"

There was no immediate answer. Only silence. Only darkness.

The dark night of the soul is often misunderstood as destruction, but I've come to see it as an initiation. It's the space where the false self is stripped away so something real can take its place. It's like falling into the void, where nothing makes sense because the framework you once relied on no longer exists. I wasn't just questioning what I believed – I was questioning *who I was.*

In that space of not knowing, I discovered something powerful: *the freedom of surrender.*

Unlearning wasn't about rejecting everything. It was about making space – space for new awareness, new possibilities, new ways of being. Some beliefs needed to be burned away entirely. Others needed to be reshaped and integrated in a way that aligned with who I was becoming.

One of the most profound lessons I learned about unlearning came during my time in Africa. There, knowledge isn't something written in stone – it's something spoken, something passed from one generation to the next through *oral tradition.* Unlike written words, which risk becoming rigid dogma, oral stories remain fluid. They evolve with time, adapting to the moment and the listener.

That's what unlearning is. It's not an abandonment of truth but an openness to its evolution. Unlearning is the realization that what served us at one stage of life may not serve us now – and that's okay. It's okay to change. It's okay to outgrow the stories we once lived by. It's okay to step into something new.

The process doesn't happen overnight. It's painful, uncomfortable, and disorienting. It's like retreating into a cave, sitting in the darkness, confronting yourself. Eventually, the darkness ends. Eventually, the light returns. And when you step out, you are not the same. You are more *you* than ever before.

Unlearning is not a one-time event. It's a cycle. You think you've reached the core of who you are, only to discover another layer waiting to be stripped away. It's a constant, beautiful unfolding. The more we allow it to happen, the more space we create – not just for ourselves, but for life itself to flow through us in ways we never imagined.

True growth isn't about adding more. It's about letting go of what no longer belongs.

RETURNING TO OUR DIVINE ESSENCE

The journey of unlearning is perhaps the most profound teacher we'll ever encounter. It strips away our certainties, challenges our deepest beliefs, and leaves us raw and vulnerable. Yet, within that vulnerability is our greatest strength.

Throughout my own dark nights, I've come to understand that we are, at our core, divine beings having a human experience. The unlearning peels away the layers that separate us from this truth, bringing us closer to our authentic selves and, by extension, to each other.

This is where the body, mind, and spirit converge. The body grounds us in the physical experience, allowing us to feel the full depth of our transformation. The mind processes and integrates these experiences, turning them into wisdom. And the spirit? The spirit guides us through the darkness, reminding us that even in our most isolated moments, we're connected to something greater.

Unity and oneness aren't just abstract concepts – they're the natural state we return to when we shed what no longer serves us. Each time we go through this cycle of learning, unlearning, and integration, we don't just transform ourselves; we contribute to the collective awakening of humanity. Every mask we remove and every truth we uncover creates ripples that extend far beyond our individual journey.

Remember that this path isn't about reaching a final destination. There will always be more layers to peel back, more truths to uncover, more moments of transformation to embrace. The divine purpose isn't about achieving perfection but staying open to the journey, remaining willing to sit in the darkness when necessary, and trusting in the light that inevitably follows.

As we close this chapter, I invite you to reflect on your own journey of unlearning. What beliefs are you ready to release? What truths are waiting to emerge? The dark night of the soul isn't something to fear; it's a sacred space where transformation becomes possible. And while the process may feel solitary, remember that you're part of a greater whole. Your journey of remembering who you are is intricately connected to the collective awakening of all beings.

In the end, the divine purpose reveals itself not in grand moments of enlightenment but in the quiet wisdom that comes from embracing both the light and the shadow, the learning and the unlearning, the breaking down and the building up. It's in this dance between opposites that we find our truth, remember our essence, and step fully into who we were always meant to be.

What You Have Unmasked

Throughout this chapter, I've peeled back another layer of illusion and stepped closer to my own divine essence. And so have you. You've started to recognize that your body, mind, and spirit are not separate —each one holds a thread in the tapestry of your purpose. You've touched the quiet wisdom underneath all the noise. You've begun to remember: you were never broken – you were becoming. This chapter brought you into the dance of unlearning, awakening, and returning home to truth.

PERSONAL LIBERATION BLUEPRINT - PART I

This is your moment to take a pause. Before you move forward, take a moment to go inward. These prompts are invitations to return to yourself. This is where wisdom becomes embodiment. Let your answers be honest, raw, and incomplete. You're not here to perform for anyone. You are here to reclaim.

Start here. Begin to unmask ...

Step 1: Identify the Mask You Wear Most Often

Purpose: Helps you become conscious of unconscious self-protection.

Which version of yourself do you present most often to the world-at work, with family, in relationships? Name it. What does this mask protect you from?

Step 2: Trace the Mask's Origin

Purpose: Bridges mask to wound – builds self-awareness and compassion.

When did this mask first appear? What moment, relationship, or pain taught you that this version of you was more 'acceptable' or 'safe'?

Step 3: Reclaim the Voice Beneath the Mask

Purpose: Moves you into self-expression and emotional risk, in a safe, written way.

What truth have you silenced because of this mask? Write one sentence that feels dangerous but authentic to say.

Step 4: Anchor Into Purpose, Not Performance

Purpose: Redirects identity from protection to purpose. Gives you clarity on your divine assignment.

If you no longer needed that mask to survive ... what would you give your energy to instead?

Step 5: Declare Your Unmasking Intention

Purpose: Integrates the work you've just done. Creates a declaration you can return to as a grounding tool.

Write an "I Am" statement that affirms your wholeness *without* the mask.

For inspiration, my "I Am" statement is: *I am the embodiment of truth, love, and light-nothing to hide, nothing to prove.*

PART II

UNMASKING THE INNER CHILD

*"If you want to understand
the adult, look at the child."*
– *Sigmund Freud*

CHAPTER 4

OUR CHILDHOOD AND THE SEEDS OF MASKING

What You Will Unmask

In this chapter, I return to the beginning – not the day I was born, but the moment my soul was shaped. I share the story of losing my mother and the moment everything changed. But this isn't just about me – it's an invitation for you to explore where your own earliest masks formed. Maybe it was the silence after a loss or the pressure to grow up too soon. If you've ever wondered why you sometimes shrink, hide, or harden, this chapter helps you trace it back to the soil where those seeds were planted. You'll begin to see that what you thought was weakness ... was really your first act of protection.

The masks we carry are an amalgamation of the moments that shape us, hardening over days, years, and even generations. Yet, of all the phases of life, our childhood is the most formative. It's the foundation, the glue that binds together so much of who we become. Our childhood is where the seeds are planted – seeds that grow into the truths we carry, the perspectives we hold, and ultimately, the masks we wear.

Much of what we experience, and how we perceive and interpret it as adults, can be traced back to those early years. It defines how we navigate life, how we react and respond to it, and how we find our "purpose" in the world.

No matter what we experience in our childhood, it's a time when the seeds of our future selves are planted and nurtured. These seeds are fed by the experiences that follow. Like a small tree, a seed grows roots, and as it's watered and nurtured by life, it either blossoms into something fruitful or turns into a weed that takes hold of our inner garden. Not everything planted in childhood is harmful; some things sustain and uplift us. But the seeds rooted in pain, fear, or misunderstanding, when left unchecked, can choke out the good and overshadow our higher potential.

Part of our journey is learning to tend to our inner garden – identifying the weeds, pulling them out at the root, and making space for the fruitful seeds to thrive.

Childhood is where our foundation is laid. The experiences of those early years shape our lives in profound ways, for better or worse. The key to growth is to look back with awareness, to honor the fruitful seeds while unearthing the weeds, and to step into the fullness of who we are meant to be.

LOSING MY BELOVED MOTHER

At just three years old, I experienced the loss of my mother. The memories of that time come to me in fragments, like pieces of a puzzle I've spent decades trying to fit together. Some memories remained buried until my thirties, only surfacing when I was ready to face them.

My mother was my world, though I didn't fully understand that until she was gone. From what I've been told, she was vibrant and full of life just six months before her death. She would constantly be by my side, working and playing with me daily. I was her miracle child – her second child, but her first to survive. Her first had died prematurely before birth, and complications during my delivery meant she couldn't have any more children after me. Perhaps that's why she poured so much love into our relationship during those brief years we had together.

The change came suddenly. Leukemia. At the time, the word meant nothing to me, but I watched as it transformed my mother from someone who could lift me high in the air to someone who couldn't even rest comfortably in her own bed. She needed to lie on hard surfaces, her body betraying her day by day.

I didn't understand what was happening to her. At three years old, how could I?

I remember one time when she was lying on the floor, I tried to play with her as I always had. But of course, she couldn't play with me like she always had.

My attempts to be with her became more and more difficult. Even though I didn't understand why we couldn't play or what was wrong,

I could feel the heartache, pain, and fear. I would still try to approach her, wanting to sit on her lap or be lifted up, only to be pulled away by well-meaning relatives. My uncle would sometimes slap my bottom and tell me to go outside, not understanding that each rejection was carving deep grooves in my young psyche. I couldn't comprehend why my mother, who had always been so engaging and playful, now seemed to be pushing me away.

The adults around us tried to protect both of us: her from physical discomfort and me from the harsh reality of what was happening. But their protection came at a cost. Each time I was pulled away from her, each moment I was told to "give Mommy space," I felt a little more disconnected, a little more confused. I watched from a distance as more and more people filled our house, their faces bearing expressions I couldn't yet understand.

During her illness, my grandmother came to help care for me. She was a stranger to me then, though she would later become my primary caregiver. I remember the confusion of having this new person in our home, trying to fill a role that, in my mind, wasn't empty. My mother was still there, physically present but increasingly distant, and I couldn't understand why everyone was acting as if things needed to be different.

When she died, I didn't have the capacity to fully grasp what that meant; I just knew that suddenly, my mother wasn't there anymore. The house filled with even more people, their voices hushed, their eyes often turning to me with a mixture of pity and concern that I would come to know well in the following years.

The immediate aftermath brought more changes than my young mind could process. My father, consumed by his own grief, fell into a deep depression. He couldn't bear to stay in the house filled with memories of my mother, so he left, adding another layer to my loss. I was left in the care of my grandmother, who, despite being a loving presence, was still essentially a stranger to me.

Our house, our home, then became a different place entirely. It felt cold and empty, and the spaces where my mother used to be seemed to echo with her absence.

I remember lying in bed at night, counting the dents and holes in the walls – a habit that would stay with me for years. The television only worked for about an hour each day, starting at 4 PM, and there wasn't much for a child to do in our community except play outside. But play had lost its luster for me; it had become associated with those painful moments of being pulled away from my mother.

During those early days after her death, people often tried to talk to me about her, but I quickly learned these conversations brought pain to the adults around me. Their eyes would well up, their voices would crack, and soon the subject would be changed. As a result, I stopped asking questions. I learned to keep my curiosity about her to myself, to bury my need to understand what had happened and who she had been.

The community rallied around us in their way, but their well-meaning attempts to help often left me feeling more isolated. They would whisper about me being "the poor boy who lost his mother," not realizing I could hear them. Their pity, though coming from a place of care, created a barrier between me and my peers. I was "different" now, and even at three years old, this was something I could understand very well.

Her absence left a void in my life. When she was gone, so too was my sense of happiness, love, and safety. In those early years, I retreated inward and sought solace in silence. Our community in Jamaica was not one for structured activities or organized entertainment. Without school work to distract me (as I didn't particularly engage with it) and with limited television access, I spent countless hours alone with my thoughts. This solitude became both a refuge and a burden, a space where I could feel the full weight of my mother's absence while also beginning to develop a connection to something deeper within myself.

Looking back now, I can see how these early experiences with loss shaped my relationship with silence and spirituality.

In those quiet moments, forced to confront an absence I couldn't fully understand, I began to develop a sensitivity to the more subtle aspects of existence. Despite my seclusion, I still felt the world around me. In fact, I felt everything deeply, with even the smallest things having a big impact on my state of being, but I masked it all behind a quiet stoicism. Though it wasn't until much later in life, when I was able to take off that mask, that I discovered that the lack of external stimulation and the depth of my loss during my childhood created a space where I could feel a connection to something beyond the physical world.

THE DAY THINGS WOULD NEVER BE THE SAME

Chad and I weren't just friends. We were *fixtures* in each other's lives, as constant as the setting sun. For two years, we made the two-mile walk home together from our school every single day, without exception. That walk wasn't just a routine – it was *ours*. A sacred space where childhood was still untouched, where the world outside our friendship didn't matter.

We didn't just talk – we moved. We raced down sidewalks, turned trees into jungle gyms, and transformed stray sticks into makeshift swords. The rhythm of our steps was as familiar as our laughter, a cadence that belonged only to us.

But that Friday … something felt different.

Even now, decades later, I struggle to explain it. There was a shift – something unspoken yet undeniable. A feeling settled deep in my gut, quiet but urgent. I *had* to stay after school.

It didn't make sense. Chad and I *never* broke tradition. But that day, the school was showing cartoons, and something inside me whispered, *"Stay."*

So I did.

Chad turned to me, confused but unfazed.

"I'll be right behind you," I told him.

Such simple words.

Who knew they'd be the last ones we'd ever share?

He left with the usual group, heading down the same path we had walked a thousand times. I stayed, watching the screen but unable to shake the unease that sat heavy in my chest.

By the time I finally walked outside, the world had changed.

I didn't see it happen, but I felt it before I even reached the street. The way the air hung thick with something *wrong*. The flashing lights. The scattered voices, some panicked, others hushed. The unmistakable sound of a siren wailing in the distance.

And then, I saw it.

The crowd. The screeching tires. The motionless figure on the pavement.

Chad.

It was like a movie scene playing out in front of me, but I wasn't watching – I was *inside* of it. A moment that should have lasted seconds stretched into eternity.

He was gone. Just like that.

And I wasn't there.

I was supposed to be there. I was *always* there.

The weight of that realization settled over me like a stone. *If I had walked with him, would it have happened? Could I have stopped it?* The questions circled endlessly in my mind, but there were no answers. Only silence. Only the crushing, inescapable truth remained that he was gone, and I was still "here."

The walk home became something entirely different after that. Every crack in the sidewalk, every fence we used to race past, and every tree we once climbed weren't just landmarks anymore. They were *memories*, frozen in time, ghosts of a friendship ripped away too soon.

At school, Chad's empty desk became a monument to absence. No one knew how to talk about it. Not our teachers. Not our parents. Not us.

Grief, especially for children, is an unspoken thing. We were expected to keep going, to adapt, to pretend that something irreversible hadn't just happened. But *everything* had changed.

The thing about childhood trauma is that it plants seeds in your consciousness. Some grow into fear. Some into detachment. Some into a quiet, gnawing understanding that life isn't as permanent as you once believed.

That day didn't just take my best friend.

It took away my sense of safety. My belief that things last. That routine means *forever*.

For years, I carried the weight of that guilt.

I thought, *"Maybe if I had been there, it wouldn't have happened. Maybe if I hadn't stayed behind, we would have walked slower, taken a different route, avoided that exact moment in time. Maybe, maybe, maybe ..."*

It wasn't until much later – years later, during a plant medicine journey – that I began to see it for what it was.

In that altered state, I saw the moment again, but this time from a different perspective. It wasn't random. It wasn't a coincidence. That feeling I had to stay behind – it wasn't an accident.

It was *protection*.

Some call it a higher self. Some say it's a guardian angel, Divine intervention, fate. But I *felt* it – clearer than I ever had before.

It wasn't something separate from me. It was *me*. The deeper, knowing part of me sensed something my conscious mind couldn't comprehend.

I had spent so much time questioning why I wasn't there. What I didn't realize was that I wasn't *meant* to be.

That realization changed me.

I finally understood that intuition – *that voice inside* – isn't just a passing thought or a coincidence. It's something real. Something ancient. Something that speaks in ways beyond words, beyond logic, beyond explanation.

And it *knows*.

That day wasn't just about loss. It was about a deeper lesson – one I wouldn't understand until much later.

When I think of Chad now, I don't focus on the accident. I don't dwell on the tragedy. I remember the walks, the laughter, and the feeling of being seen and understood. I carry that with me because while that day was the end of *his story* in this world, it wasn't the end of *his impact*.

It lives on in me. It lives on every time I listen to my intuition. It lives on in the way I cherish the people I love. It lives on in the way I *know*, beyond a shadow of a doubt, that we are guided in ways we don't always understand.

And now, through these words, through this story, *his memory lives on in you too.*

These are the lessons that stayed with me …

1. **Intuition is real. Trust it.** The pull you feel, the nudge in your gut, the inexplicable *knowing* – it's not random. It's your inner guidance, and it knows things your mind cannot yet see.

2. **Time is not promised.** We assume we have time. That we can finish conversations later. That we'll always have another walk home, another game, another tomorrow. But life can change in a heartbeat.

3. **Grief is not something to "get over." It's something to carry with you.** Loss doesn't disappear. It becomes part of you. But instead of weighing you down, it can shape you, deepen you, remind you to love harder, to live fully, to *listen* when something inside you says, *Stay.*

RAINING CANDY!

My childhood did not shape me solely through its challenges and losses. Some seeds planted during those years came from positive experiences and grew into strengths that have carried me throughout my life. Among them, for example, was a natural entrepreneurial spirit, something that became a defining part of who I am.

It started small, as these things often do. I didn't realize it at the time, but running a candy business out of a fanny pack was my first real entrepreneurial venture. It wasn't born out of ambition for wealth but out of necessity. I didn't want to burden my grandmother by asking her for extra money, knowing our household only had just enough to get by. So, I found a way to earn it myself.

At first, it was simple: buy candy, sell it to kids in the neighborhood, and keep track of the profits. But it quickly became more than that. The lessons started coming thick and fast. I learned how to manage inventory, figuring out which items sold the fastest and what I should buy more of. I discovered a pricing strategy, setting my rates to stay competitive while ensuring I made enough to reinvest in more stock. I even mastered a bit of team building, offering my friends a 25% commission on sales to expand my reach.

By the time I was 13, I was grappling with concepts most adults struggle with, like accounting, motivation, and even international sourcing. When local suppliers couldn't keep up with my demand, I convinced my uncle in Canada to send me larger shipments. That first payment to him felt monumental, a sign that I could think beyond the limitations of my circumstances.

My ventures weren't limited to candy. Around the same time, I turned our living room into a makeshift movie theater.

Armed with a VCR, two movies, and a bit of improvisation, I charged 25 cents for admission and gave my neighbors something fun to do when there was usually "nothing to do." But it wasn't just about the money; it was about creating something that brought people together and put smiles on their faces.

Years later, I stood at the bobsled track in Whistler, Canada, the very one featured in *Cool Runnings*, a movie I had shown countless times in my little theater. It was a moment of profound reflection, connecting the boy who charged 25 cents for movie viewings with the man I had become.

Those early experiences were about transformation. A fanny pack of candy became a lesson in business management. A simple VCR became a tool for creating community. And necessity became the fertile ground for creativity and resourcefulness. Whether selling candy or letting people come and enjoy a movie for a few hours, those early ventures were more than just ways to earn money. They were lessons in independence, problem-solving, and resilience, where each small victory, whether it was buying my own school supplies or expanding my candy sales to other schools, reinforced the belief that I could create opportunities where others saw none.

Not every seed planted in childhood grows into something positive, but that one did. Those early ventures taught me not just how to earn money but how to see possibilities, solve problems, and create value. They showed me that even when circumstances are limited, the potential for growth is always there.

As I stated in the beginning, masks are not always bad; they are needed. "Ike the Entrepreneur" mask is a perfect example of those positive masks, one that was developed in my childhood and has served me long into my adulthood. Without that formative childhood spirit, without that mask, I may never have had the chance to write this book now.

What You Have Unmasked

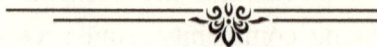

At the end of this chapter, I've begun grieving what I once buried, and you've been invited to do the same. You've started to trace your oldest stories, your deepest adaptations, and your most sacred inner child. You may now understand that your earliest survival patterns weren't failures – they were intelligence. They were love. This chapter cracked the shell just enough for you to begin healing where it all began.

CHAPTER 5

CALCIFIED MASKS OF CHILDHOOD & OUR SOULS LEARNING TO HIDE

What You Will Unmask

In this chapter, I pull back the layers on some of the most painful disguises I've worn – the ones shaped in childhood, hardened over time, and reinforced by trauma and silence. But this isn't just about my journey. It's about yours, too. If you've ever wondered why certain patterns still grip you or why emotional triggers feel so intense, it's often because the mask is no longer a choice ... It's become a reflex. You'll begin to recognize how shame has shaped your voice, your relationships, and even your sense of worth. And as you do, you'll be empowered to start loosening what once felt locked in place.

The shadows of our childhood experiences lurk beneath the surface of our adult lives, shaping our behaviors in ways we often fail to recognize. Those masks, born from early wounds, protective instincts, and survival mechanisms, initially serve a purpose.

They shield us from pain. But over time, they harden, calcify, and ultimately hinder our growth and authentic expression.

Understanding these shadows requires a journey back to their origins. We must examine how early experiences planted seeds that have grown into the adult patterns and behaviors we now display automatically.

For example, when a child loses a parent or experiences inconsistent emotional support, they often develop protective mechanisms that persist into adulthood. In my own experience, losing my mother at age three created deep-seated patterns around abandonment. While I didn't consciously remember many details, the impact manifested in how I responded to and perceived rejection. Each "no" felt like abandonment. Each unfulfilled promise triggered that original wound.

It wasn't until I reached the age of 33 – the same age at which my mother passed – that these memories and patterns began to surface, demanding attention and healing. That symbolic age became a catalyst for examining what had been buried for so long.

A more common origin for many of our childhood masks is bullying. Bullying is so toxic because it doesn't just affect the surface; it burrows deep into a person's sense of self, shaping their identity in painful ways. To me, it's less of a fertilizer and more like salt. It gets poured over those inner child wounds, seeping deep into the soil of who we are, drying it out, and making those wounds grow in ways they shouldn't.

For a child, bullying can feel like confirmation that they're not good enough, that they need to hide or shrink just to survive. It makes them wary of standing out, fearing judgment or rejection. To defend themselves, children create a mask that doesn't shape how they grow but instead contorts it so that they can protect themselves.

Over time, this fear stunts their growth, like a tree that isn't properly watered or cared for. If a child's true self is mocked, laughed at, or crushed, that part of their "tree" withers, leaving parts of who they are undeveloped and unable to bear fruit.This damage doesn't stay confined to childhood; it ripples into adulthood, influencing relationships, confidence, and even the ability to embrace opportunities.

I remember the sting of being the kid picked last for the football team. While not outright bullying, it felt like a silent judgment each time. Standing there, waiting for my name, I could feel my confidence shrink with each passing choice. That experience made me hesitant in countless other situations, always second-guessing whether I belonged or was good enough.

But there was one remarkable day when, out of nowhere, I got picked third. I don't know what changed – maybe someone took a chance, or maybe they saw something in me. That day, I gave it everything. Every kick, every pass, I was on fire. I became the best player on the field not because I suddenly learned new skills but because I had something to prove. **For once, I felt seen, and that small shift in perception lit a fire in me that hadn't burned before.** Looking back, it's a reminder of how much those little moments shape us, for better or worse.

Turning to you …

1. What childhood experiences might still be influencing your behaviors, fears, or self-perception today?

2. What protective masks have you created to shield yourself, and are they still serving you – or is it time to let them go?

SHAME: THE JAILER

Shame is one of the most deeply rooted emotions we experience as humans. It thrives on self-criticism, constantly whispering that we're never good enough. It fuels people-pleasing behaviors, pushing us to put others' needs above our own to gain approval or avoid conflict. It leaves us with a sense of being broken or flawed in ways that feel irreparable, convincing us that we're unworthy of love, success, or happiness.

What makes shame particularly insidious is its subtlety. It rarely announces itself loudly. Instead, it creeps in quietly, embedding itself in small, vulnerable moments throughout our lives. Over time, it fundamentally reshapes how we see ourselves and interact with the world.

Shame rarely appears out of nowhere. It often has roots in past experiences, societal expectations, or careless words spoken during childhood. The things we overhear, the ways we're treated, or the subtle comparisons to others all leave an imprint. A harsh word from a parent or teacher, the sting of exclusion by peers, or even societal ideals about what it means to be "good enough" can plant seeds of shame that grow quietly over the years, creating long-lasting patterns of self-doubt, fear, and disconnection.

Above all, shame teaches us to hide. It tells us that if others saw the real us – the unpolished, imperfect, vulnerable us – we'd face rejection. So, we begin to cover up. We avoid vulnerability at all costs, pretending to have it all together while silently battling feelings of inadequacy. We hide parts of ourselves that we fear others won't accept, creating distance in relationships and disconnecting from our own authenticity. This constant performance becomes exhausting, yet the thought of being seen feels even more terrifying.

Shame doesn't stop there. It generates powerful patterns of self-blame. When things go wrong, we internalize the responsibility, believing it's our fault. This might stem from childhood environments where blame was disproportionately placed on us, or where we were made to feel that our worth depended on being "good" or "perfect." As adults, this pattern plays out in relationships, work, and personal challenges. It keeps us stuck, replaying mistakes in our minds and holding ourselves to impossible standards.

Shame also fosters an inferiority complex. It convinces us that everyone else is more capable, deserving, or successful, leaving us to feel small and insignificant. This sense of being "less than" makes it hard to celebrate our own achievements or even recognise them. We may find ourselves constantly comparing, always falling short in our own eyes. When success does come, shame tells us it's a fluke or that we somehow don't deserve it.

All of this is amplified when it begins in childhood.

A powerful memory from my own childhood comes to mind here. A neighbor had found a small kitten and, for some reason, put it in a bag and started swinging it around. He was violent. It was inhumane.

I remember feeling anger, horror, sadness all tangled together. Though I was just a kid, and he was much bigger than me, I couldn't stand by watching. I ran over and confronted him. We ended up getting into a fight, and he shoved me hard and threw the kitten into the air. I was crying, really crying, and all the other kids started laughing. Not at what happened to the cat, but at me. Because I was crying. Because I cared.

That moment taught me something painful about the world. I realized how far removed people could be from tenderness, from empathy, from simply feeling. I grew up in a community where men didn't cry. I never saw it. Emotions were framed as weakness, especially in boys.

So I stopped crying after that. I shut down a part of myself because I didn't want to be seen as soft or laughable. I tried to be tough, but it never truly fit.

Years later, I was watching *Toy Story*, of all the things, and unexpectedly broke down five minutes into the film. I cried for almost an hour. That moment was cathartic. It cracked something open in me and made me ask, *Why was I ever ashamed of feeling deeply?* Why was that framed as weakness? Why was society making me feel this way…

This played out further when I had kids, especially my son. I started to see that same cycle trying to repeat. I caught myself saying the same things that were said to me: "You're too sensitive," "Toughen up." And it hit me. I was becoming the voice that once silenced me. That's when I knew I had to break the pattern. I had to show him that being sensitive isn't something to fix or overcome; it's something to protect, something to honor.

As children, we're impressionable, and the messages we receive – whether intentional or not – become the lens through which we view the world. A child who is criticised harshly might grow into an adult who constantly second-guesses themselves. A child whose emotional needs are unmet may learn to suppress their feelings, leading to struggles with vulnerability and intimacy later in life. Those early moments of shame create patterns that shape our thoughts, behaviours, and relationships and are then reinforced by societal expectations.

Society tells us what it means to be successful, attractive, or worthy, and those ideals are impossible to meet fully. When we fall short, shame steps in to remind us of our perceived inadequacies. It tells us that we'll only be worthy if we try harder, achieve more, or fit into the mold others have created. This creates a cycle of striving and self-criticism, leaving little room for self-compassion or acceptance.

However, when we understand that these patterns of self-criticism, people-pleasing, and avoidance stem from deeply rooted beliefs, not truths, we can begin to challenge them. Healing requires courage: the courage to face our vulnerabilities, examine our pasts, and rewrite the narratives shame has created. Only then can we move toward a more compassionate and authentic way of being, unburdened by the weight of feeling "not enough."

The masks we develop don't just affect our emotional responses; they fundamentally shape how we move through the world. Some become fiercely self-reliant, refusing to depend on others or ask for help. While this self-sufficiency might appear as strength, it often masks a deep fear of vulnerability and connection. The shadow side emerges in isolation, difficulty trusting others, and a critical nature that focuses on what's missing rather than what's present. This self-reliance can drive entrepreneurial success and personal achievement but at the cost of genuine connection and interdependence.

MULTIPLE MASKS, MULTIPLE IMPACTS ...

The protective masks we wear can take various forms, each with its own hidden cost.

Financial insecurity masks often develop in those who experienced childhood poverty or resource scarcity. Even after achieving financial stability later in life, these people might maintain a scarcity mindset, hoarding resources and overworking despite having "enough." This state of living in perpetual preparation for loss prevents them from enjoying present abundance. It often manifests in compulsive saving or an inability to enjoy their financial success and difficulty *feeling* financially secure even when they are objectively stable.

Social anxiety masks frequently stem from early experiences of bullying or peer rejection. Something as seemingly minor as being picked last for the team can plant seeds of self-doubt that bloom into adult fears of judgment and social avoidance. While these masks originally were protection from further hurt, they now limit authentic connection and expression. These masks can impact more than our social abilities, including affecting career advancement, relationship formation, and overall life satisfaction.

Perfectionism masks often develop in children with critical or controlling parents. The "helicopter parent" phenomenon, though born from love and protection, can create adults who fear making mistakes and constantly seek external validation. These individuals might struggle with decision-making, paralyzed by the fear of making wrong choices. It's a mask that might initially prevent and protect against failure, but it also stifles creativity, spontaneity, and genuine growth.

But perhaps most insidious are **the masks of emotional poverty**. These masks are worn by individuals who grew up in emotionally volatile environments. For these individuals, it becomes difficult to trust the stability of relationships or distinguish genuine connections from superficial ones. Even those from materially wealthy backgrounds can wear these masks if their emotional needs went unmet. The result is often a pattern of unstable relationships, difficulty with emotional intimacy, or an inability to recognize and trust authentic connections.

These are only a handful of the masks we can develop in childhood and that we carry with us into adulthood. There are countless others, and the impact of these masks becomes particularly evident in how we relate to others and ourselves. In classroom settings, for instance, a child might develop another mask: **the mask of false understanding**, nodding along when confused to avoid shame or attention. This pattern can persist into adulthood, manifesting as difficulty asking for help or clarification in professional settings. The fear of appearing incompetent becomes a barrier to learning and growth.

It is, however, crucial to understand that these masks weren't arbitrary choices; they served as essential survival mechanisms during vulnerable periods of our lives. A child who learns to be hypervigilant in an unstable environment isn't making a conscious choice; they're adapting to ensure their safety and survival. Their mask protects them; it served them well, but may now manifest as anxiety and inability to relax even in secure situations.

The key to understanding your masks is to look at how they were made, to look at the circumstances surrounding your upbringing. What happened when you were a child, and how did you respond or react? Understanding this, you can then begin to understand how these masks evolved into the habits and patterns that you have as an adult so that you can begin to remove the ones that are no longer serving you.

1. Which masks have shaped the way you move through the world, and are they still protecting you – or are they keeping you from something greater?

2. What parts of yourself have been hidden beneath these masks, waiting to be seen, understood, and finally set free?

MASKS THAT SPAN
BEYOND OUR LIFETIMES

The intergenerational nature of these masks adds another layer of complexity. As parents, we might unconsciously project our own wounds onto our children, attempting to protect them from experiences that hurt us. For example, seeing a child's gentle, loving nature might trigger our own memories of vulnerability, leading us to push them toward "toughness" out of fear. This projection, though well-intentioned, can create new masks in the next generation.

These patterns run deep, often operating below the level of conscious awareness until something triggers their recognition. For me, reaching the age of my mother's passing became a catalyst for examining these hidden influences. It's often not until we face similar situations or reach significant life stages that we begin to question why we react in certain ways or make particular choices.

The work of addressing these masked elements begins with recognition – understanding that many of our current struggles trace back to these early "protective mechanisms." This awareness doesn't come easily; it often requires us to sit with uncomfortable truths and examine patterns we've long accepted as "just who we are." The process involves not only identifying these masks but also understanding the meanings we've attached to past experiences and how they continue to shape our present reality.

While these masks served a purpose in our past, acknowledging their presence in our present allows us to begin the work of integration and healing. This doesn't mean completely discarding these protective mechanisms – some aspects may still serve valuable purposes.

Instead, it's about bringing consciousness to our patterns, understanding their origins, and making intentional choices about how we want to move forward.

The journey of unmasking isn't about reaching a destination of perfect authenticity but rather about developing awareness of our protective patterns and choosing consciously how we want to show up in the world. Through this process, we can begin to transform these shadows from unconscious limitations into conscious choices, creating space for more authentic and fulfilled ways of being.

What You Have Unmasked

By the end of this chapter, I've begun dismantling the armor that once felt like my only protection. And perhaps you've begun to feel yours crack open, too. Are you seeing how masks can calcify around pain, shame, and survival – and how it's possible to break them down with compassion, awareness, and courage? This chapter gave you language for the hurt you've buried ... and a doorway to begin releasing it.

CHAPTER 6

ATTACHMENT MASKS THROUGH ATTACHMENT STYLES

What You Will Unmask

This chapter explores how childhood attachment wounds don't just shape our relationships – they shape the very masks we wear to survive them. If you've ever wondered why you pull away, cling, shut down, or overfunction in relationships, this chapter will give you language for those patterns. Together, we'll unpack how attachment styles – anxious, avoidant, secure, and disorganized – create masks of need, control, fear, or invisibility. You'll start seeing that these behaviors weren't personality flaws ...they were survival strategies.

From the moment we are born, we seek connection – attachment. Attachment is the invisible thread that ties us to one another. It also shapes how we see the world, how we navigate relationships, and ultimately, how we learn to protect ourselves. When our attachment needs are met consistently, we develop a foundation of trust and security. But when those needs are met inconsistently – or not at all – we create masks to survive in a world of uncertainty or insecurity.

In many ways, the masks we wear are direct reflections of our attachment styles. They are defense mechanisms, shields we put up to protect ourselves from repeating the wounds of the past.

Understanding your attachment style can be a powerful step in unmasking. It helps uncover the hidden forces driving your behaviors, your fears, and your patterns of connection and disconnection. There are four primary attachment styles.

1. **Secure Attachment:** The Unmasked Self

Children with secure attachments grow up feeling safe, seen, and supported. Their caregivers respond to their needs with consistency and warmth, teaching them that the world is a reliable place. As adults, they navigate relationships with ease. They trust others, express emotions openly, and feel comfortable both giving and receiving love.

A securely attached person has little need for masks. They don't hide their emotions out of fear of rejection, nor do they build walls to keep people at a distance. They move through life with a sense of wholeness, aligned with their inner child rather than at war with it.

But even those with secure attachments can develop protective masks later in life, especially in response to trauma or betrayal. The key difference is their ability to recognize these masks and remove them without losing their sense of self.

2. **Anxious Attachment:** The Mask of Overcompensation

Anxiously attached children often experience inconsistent caregiving – sometimes their needs are met, other times they are ignored. This unpredictability fosters a deep fear of abandonment. As adults, they crave closeness but often feel insecure in relationships, needing constant reassurance of their worth and love.

This attachment style can lead to a relentless pursuit of validation. Those who wear this mask may become people-pleasers, perfectionists, or emotional caretakers, believing if they give enough or prove themselves worthy, they won't be abandoned. They often struggle with setting boundaries, over-apologize, seek external validation, and feel anxious in relationships. Their need to be needed or wanted can drive them to self-sacrifice, sometimes at their own expense.

Beneath the mask is a longing for security that external validation can never truly fill. Unmasking for an anxiously attached person involves learning self-soothing, setting boundaries, and meeting their own emotional needs rather than relying on others to define their worth.

3. Avoidant Attachment: The Mask of Independence

Avoidantly attached children grow up in environments where emotional expression is discouraged or met with indifference. Their caregivers may have been distant, emotionally unavailable, or dismissive of their needs. In response, these children learn to suppress their emotions, relying only on themselves.

As adults, they become fiercely independent, wearing a mask of self-sufficiency as a shield that keeps others at a safe distance. They may pride themselves on being "low maintenance" in relationships, but beneath that exterior is often a fear of vulnerability. They withdraw themselves from real attachment out of fear of being hurt or a lack of understanding.

This mask isn't about genuine independence; it's about self-protection. The avoidant person unconsciously believes that needing others is dangerous because, in their past, those needs were unmet. Their journey toward unmasking involves learning that vulnerability isn't a threat; it's a bridge to deeper connection.

4. Disorganized Attachment: The Mask of Chaos

Disorganized attachment develops in children who grow up in environments where their caregiver is both a source of comfort and fear. This often happens in cases of abuse, neglect, or highly unpredictable parenting. These children don't develop a clear strategy for connection, and as they grow up, they crave closeness but fear intimacy, leading to a cycle of push and pull.

As adults, they struggle with emotional regulation and trust. Their relationships often feel turbulent – one moment, they're deeply attached, the next, they're pushing people away. They may swing between anxious and avoidant tendencies, never quite feeling safe in closeness but also fearing abandonment. They have difficulty trusting both themselves and others, never truly able to commit to anything or anyone as their self-sabotaging behaviors often get in their way.

The disorganized attachment mask is one of the hardest to unmask because it's rooted in a conflicting belief: *I want connection, but I don't trust it.* The journey toward healing involves deep inner work: learning to build trust in themselves and others, processing past trauma, and creating an internal sense of safety.

HOW ATTACHMENT STYLES RELATE TO THE CHILDHOOD MASKS WE WEAR

Each attachment style is tied to a Childhood Mask. These masks, once necessary for survival as we learned to cope when our emotional needs weren't met, now act as barriers to true connection and wholeness.

When we recognize the patterns, we gain the power to change them. Unmasking isn't about placing blame or developing resentment of our past; it's about understanding how our past shaped us and choosing how we want to move forward.

Unmasking childhood wounds begins with awareness. Breaking free from attachment-driven masks takes time. You must give your grace. Don't judge yourself; acknowledge your masks with compassion. Ask yourself: What mask am I wearing? What am I protecting myself from with this mask?

The goal isn't to force yourself into a new attachment style overnight. It's to bring consciousness to your patterns, allowing yourself to soften, to trust, and to connect in healthier ways.

Here's where to start:

1. **Awareness** – Recognize your attachment style and the masks it has created.

2. **Inner Child Work** – Reconnect with the part of you that first developed these defenses.

3. **Self-Regulation** – Learn how to soothe yourself rather than relying on external validation.

4. **Challenge the Narrative** – Ask yourself: Is this belief serving me, or is it a story from my past?

5. **Build Secure Relationships** – Surround yourself with people who support your unmasking process.

Attachment styles aren't destiny. They're just starting points. The more conscious we become, the more we can shift, allowing ourselves to unmask and experience life without the weight of the past dictating our future.

What would you say is your attachment style? How has this affected you and your relationships …?

RECOMMENDATIONS

On my journey, I've come across numerous resources that have deepened my understanding and opened my eyes to new possibilities and realities. Some have helped me to better understand where my masks came from and how to remove the masks that no longer served me. However, knowing where to start can be overwhelming. So, to help navigate the overwhelm, below are some of my recommendations to help you discover and understand some of the masks of your childhood.

"Adult Attachment Styles: Relationship with Parenting" by Mehak Goel[1]

This paper examines the connection between adult romantic behaviors and parenting methods, exploring how early caregiver interactions influence attachment styles and adult relationship behaviors.

"Assessing the Consequences of Childhood Trauma on Behavioral Issues and Mental Health Outcomes" by Myriam V. Thoma et al.[2]

This editorial explores the relationship between childhood trauma and various health outcomes across the lifespan, including behavioral issues and mental health outcomes.

"Effects of Helicopter Parenting, Tiger Parenting and Inhibitory Control on the Development of Children's Anxiety and Depressive Symptoms" by Runzhu Zhang & Zhenhong Wang[3]

This study examines how helicopter and tiger parenting styles affect children's anxiety and depressive symptoms and how children's internal inhibitory control moderates these effects.

"The Effects of Parenting Styles and Childhood Attachment Patterns on Intimate Relationships" by Neal, J., & Frick-Horbury, D.[4]

This study investigates how authoritative, authoritarian, and permissive parenting styles parallel secure, avoidant, and ambivalent attachment styles and how these influence intimate relationships.

"Tiger/Attachment/Helicopter Parenting: Searching for Truth Among the Books and the Blogs" by David Rettew[5]

This explores the scientific basis for various popular parenting styles, including helicopter and tiger parenting, and maps them onto authoritative, authoritarian, and permissive categories.

What You Have Unmasked

Here, I traced the link between how I learned to attach as a child and how I learned to hide. You've likely seen pieces of yourself, too. The way you show up in love, leadership, and even conflict now makes more sense, doesn't it?.
You've begun loosening the grip of old protection systems that no longer serve your becoming. This chapter gave you clarity and permission to stop blaming yourself for the ways you once tried to feel safe.

---

[1] https://www.iosrjournals.org/iosr-jhss/papers/Vol.29-Issue11/Ser-11/G2911114954.pdf

[2] https://www.frontiersin.org/research-topics/27294/assessing-the-consequences-of-childhood-trauma-on-behavioral-issues-and-mental-health-outcomes/magazine

[3] https://pubmed.ncbi.nlm.nih.gov/38401004/

[4] https://go.gale.com/ps/i.do?id=GALE%7CA79370572&sid=googleScholar&v=2.1&it=r&linkaccess=abs&issn=00941956&p=HRCA&sw=w&userGroupName=anon%7E67e5c5&aty=open-web-entry

[5] https://doi.org/10.1093/oso/9780197550977.003.0003

CHAPTER 7

LETTING OUR CHILDHOOD UNMASK

What You Will Unmask

In this chapter, I begin the delicate, courageous work of healing the childhood self – the version of me who first learned to hide. You'll be invited into this space with me, not just to look back but to meet those younger versions of yourself with compassion. If you've ever struggled with guilt, buried memories, or a feeling that something "back there" is still unfinished, this is your permission to begin tending to it. This chapter doesn't just teach healing- it lets you experience it.

The process of unmasking starts with looking back. We can't move forward without understanding where we came from – how the beliefs we hold, the behaviors we default to, and the patterns we repeat were shaped long before we had the awareness to question them.

For me, that moment came at age 33.

I was convinced I would die at the same age as my mother, and that belief had shaped everything. It was the design for how I lived, how I worked, how I planned. I pushed myself to check every box as early as possible.

I wanted to get married young, start my family young, and build whatever wealth I needed to build young.

I felt this subconscious pressure of time. Then 33 came. And I woke up. And I was still alive.

I remember sitting with that reality. I had been so certain I wouldn't make it past that age. But there I was. That was the moment I realized I had been living by a script that wasn't mine. And suddenly, I had to ask: *What now?*

I started looking back at every belief I had inherited, every assumption I had never questioned. I asked myself: "What do I actually want? What do I actually believe?"

That's when I started getting into trouble – when I started questioning everything, challenging everything.

That was the beginning of the dark night of the soul.

Because once you start pulling at those threads, everything unravels. You realize that so much of what you thought was truth was just conditioning. You see how deeply embedded the masks are, how they shape not just how we show up in the world but how we see ourselves. And to break free, to realign with our natural, truest self, we have to burn it all down.

That moment of realization looks different for everyone. But the process is always the same; it starts with a question: "What is this life I'm living? Am I happy? What is true happiness? Have I ever felt it?"

And then it deepens:

"How do I define my own success? My own peace? My own self?"

That's when the shift happens.

That's when you realize that nothing you've defined up to this point was ever truly yours. The beliefs, the rules, the limitations – they were given to you.

They were shaped by family, by culture, by school, by religion ... And once you see it, you can't unsee it.

But that's when you start rewriting your story.

Unmasking the childhood self is about peeling back the layers and seeing the mechanisms that have been running your life without your conscious permission. It's about reclaiming your own definitions, your own truth, your own way of being in the world.

The work isn't easy, but it's the only way to become truly free and sovereign.

STEPS TOWARD ALLOWING OURSELVES TO UNMASK

Unmasking the Inner child is a therapeutic process focused on reconnecting with and nurturing the part of oneself that retains the emotions, memories, and experiences from childhood. From the moment we enter this world, we're absorbing everything – spoken and unspoken rules, expectations, fears, and limitations.

Some of these serve us, keeping us safe and helping us navigate the world. But many of them are nothing more than conditioned responses, adaptations to environments that no longer exist. They become ingrained so deeply that we mistake them for truth.

Our "inner child" represents these early life experiences, the conditioning that often carries unresolved traumas, unmet needs, and beliefs that affect our adult lives. But healing this part of ourselves can lead to emotional freedom and increased self-acceptance.

As we unmask, we start addressing the seeds planted in childhood, reinterpreting their effects and creating new meanings. We understand that many of our fears, insecurities, and limitations we carry often didn't start with us, and the new meaning we give to those things forms the foundation for new beliefs, which then shape new experiences.

Whenever we feel like something is missing, like we've ticked all the boxes on the outside, but inside, there's an emptiness, that's when childhood wounds start whispering to us. Sometimes, it's not a whisper; it's a roar. It's triggered by something big: losing someone you love, having a near-death experience, or even just sitting still long enough for the silence to get uncomfortable. And it's not about age. I've met teenagers who are deeply aligned, awake to who they are in ways that blow my mind. But for most of us, it's these moments that force us to look deeper.

It's a constant process of tuning – realigning our internal compass to match where we are on the journey. What feels true at 33 may evolve by the time we're 43, and it will likely shift again at 63. There's no fixed destination, only a direction. The journey is about continuously moving toward our "True North," unconsciously adjusting and realigning as we grow and change.

ADDRESSING THE INNER CHILDHOOD MASKS

As I have previously discussed, everyone's experiences and processes will be different. There is no one "one-size-fits-all" solution. However, I have tried to give you a blueprint that can take you through the core steps of the process. At each stage, there is no right or wrong answer; it is a chance for you to explore your own childhood, uncover your own masks, and bring yourself closer to your true self.

1. Acknowledge Your Inner Child

The first and most critical step is recognition. Your inner child still exists within you, holding onto past experiences – both joyful and painful. The wounds you carry in adulthood are often reflections of what that child endured. These unresolved experiences can show up in different ways, but acknowledging the inner child begins by saying: *"I see you. I hear you. You matter."* It's about offering the presence and validation that may have been missing when you were younger.

2. Identify Triggers and Unresolved Imprints

Healing requires awareness of your triggers. Those moments when you feel an emotional reaction that seems disproportionate to the situation. Maybe rejection hits you harder than it should, or criticism sends you into a spiral of self-doubt. These are signals, breadcrumbs leading back to past wounds.

Ask yourself:

- When did I first feel this way?

- What memory comes to mind when I sit with this emotion?

- What did I need in that moment that I didn't receive?

Tracing these patterns back to their origin gives you clarity on what your inner child has been carrying all these years.

3. Express and Release Suppressed Emotions

For many, their childhood wounds were never fully expressed. Maybe they were taught to "be strong" or "get over it." Maybe there was no safe space to process sadness, fear, or anger. Those emotions didn't vanish – they were just stored, waiting for release.

Maybe you are one of those people, and if so, that's okay. If not, that's also okay. What's important to remember is that healing happens when we stop suppressing and start feeling.

There are a lot of different ways that you can express and release these emotions, and we should make the effort to look for healthy ways to express ourselves. For example, you can revisit those memories in writing, expressing the things you never got to say, do, or feel. You don't have to do anything with it, but taking the time to revisit and reframe the narrative with the freedom of expression allows you to externalize what you've internalized.

4. Reparent Yourself with Compassion

If your childhood lacked emotional safety, structure, or nurturing, you now have the opportunity to provide those things for yourself. Reparenting is the process of giving your inner child what they never received.

How to reparent yourself:

- **Practice self-compassion** – Speak to yourself as you would to a small child. Replace self-criticism with words of kindness and encouragement.

- **Establish boundaries** – Honor your needs by setting clear limits in relationships, protecting your time and energy.

- **Affirm your worth** – Rewrite limiting beliefs: *I am safe. I am loved. I am worthy.*

Reparenting is about becoming the adult your younger self needed – patient, loving, and present.

5. Engage in Play and Joyful Expression

Healing the inner child isn't just about addressing pain; it's also about reconnecting with joy. As children, we were naturally creative, playful, and curious, but over time, responsibilities and societal expectations often stifled that sense of wonder.

Think back to what lit you up as a child:

- Did you love drawing, dancing, or climbing trees?

- Did you spend hours lost in stories or making up adventures?

- What activities made you feel free?

Now, take the time to imagine how those things would look in your life right now. If you loved art or music, maybe you could pick up a paintbrush or learn a new instrument. If you loved the outdoors, why not make time to explore somewhere new? If you love stories, why not try to write your own, or if you don't feel like writing, why not dive into a new book and escape on a new adventure?

Reintroducing these experiences into your life is essential. It signals to your inner child that they are safe to exist, that they are allowed to take up space, that the things that once mattered still do, and that life isn't just about surviving; it's about living.

5. Unmasking Through Connection

While inner child work is deeply personal, it doesn't have to be done alone. Healing is magnified in safe relationships, whether with close friends, a partner, a therapist, or a spiritual guide.

Being truly seen and accepted by another person creates an experience many of us longed for as children. It's the experience of being loved without conditions, without performance, just as you are.

When you surround yourself with people who nurture your growth, it's as if your inner child finally gets to receive the love they always deserved.

REFLECTIONS FROM THE INNOCENCE WE LEFT BEHIND

Unmasking the effects of our inner child is not about erasing the past; it's about reinterpreting it, understanding its effects, and freeing ourselves from the unconscious patterns that hold us back. The child we once were is still within us, influencing the way we love, trust, fear, and react. But when we bring awareness to these patterns – when we sit with our younger selves, acknowledge their pain, and rewrite the narratives that no longer serve us – we begin the process of true healing.

For me, forgiving Ike the Kid meant understanding that he created stories to make sense of a world he didn't fully understand. It also meant forgiving my mother, not because she did anything wrong but because I had unknowingly carried the weight of her absence in a way that distorted my perception of love and connection. She wanted to lift me up, to hold me close, but her body wouldn't let her. And when I saw that – truly saw it – I was able to let go of the resentment I didn't even realize I had been carrying.

When we're children, our minds are wired for survival. We don't just experience the world; we assign meaning to everything that happens. If a parent is distant, we assume it's because we weren't enough. If we experience rejection, we believe it means we are unworthy of love. These stories become our internal programming, shaping how we move through life long after childhood has ended. And because they were formed at a time when we didn't yet have the capacity to understand the bigger picture, they are often incomplete, distorted, or just plain wrong.

That's why the process of unmasking isn't about blaming the past; it's about seeing it clearly. It's about stepping outside of those childhood interpretations and recognizing them for what they are: survival mechanisms, not truths. Once we see this, we gain the power to rewrite our own narrative.

By reframing our past, we give ourselves the chance to finally choose to be who we want to be – and who we truly are.

Many of us walk through life making decisions based on childhood wounds, whether we realize it or not. We chase validation, avoid vulnerability, or build walls around ourselves because, on some level, we're still operating from a place of self-protection. But when we heal, when we consciously integrate our past instead of running from it, we make different choices. We stop acting out of fear and start acting out of truth.

And here's the thing: this process doesn't just transform us. It ripples outward into every relationship we have. If you're a parent, your healing directly impacts your children and eventually extends to their children. When you do the work of unmasking, you're not just breaking cycles for yourself; you're breaking them for future generations. If you don't address your wounds, your children will inherit them, just as you inherited wounds from your own parents. The difference is that you now have the awareness to change that cycle.

Imagine what it would feel like to live without those invisible chains: to experience love without fear, to pursue your goals without the weight of old stories holding you back, to step into every moment as your whole, sovereign self. That is what this work is about. It's not easy. It requires courage, deep reflection, and a willingness to sit with discomfort. But with each step, you reclaim something that was always yours: your right to live as your fullest, most authentic self.

The journey of unmasking is lifelong; when you think you've peeled back the final layer, another one reveals itself. There will be moments where old wounds resurface, where you're triggered in ways you thought you'd moved past. That's normal. The difference is that now, you have tools. Now, you know how to listen, how to sit with the emotions, and how to offer yourself what you need. Growth never stops, but neither does the opportunity to step deeper into who you are meant to be.

What You Have Unmasked

By the time you close this chapter, you'll have reached inward, not just backward. I've met parts of myself I once avoided, and I believe you have too. You've unearthed tenderness where there was tension, innocence where there was shame. You've started to see that healing the child within isn't a return to weakness – it's a return to wholeness. This is the moment your past starts empowering your future.

PERSONAL LIBERATION BLUEPRINT – PART II

The masks we wear, often formed in childhood, are designed to shield us from abandonment, shame, and pain. To reclaim power, we must meet the wounded child within. Here is your opportunity. This turns emotional reflection into *identity repair.* You are walking away with a new internal contract. That's when this book you are holding stops being content and becomes **initiation.**

Step 1: Meet Your Inner Child

"Picture yourself between the ages of 4 and 8. Where are you? What are you doing? What emotion is most present in that memory?"

Purpose: Initiates emotional connection-makes the abstract inner child real.

Step 2: Identify the Moment the Child Learned to Hide

"What was the moment-spoken or unspoken-where you felt unsafe to be fully yourself? What did you start hiding from the world after that?"

Purpose: Brings clarity to the wound that created the mask.

Step 3: Write a Message *from* the Child

"What would your younger self say to you now? Without filters. Let their voice speak-messy, magical, or mad."

Purpose: Opens emotional channels. Creates intimacy between present self and past self.

Step 4: Re-parent With Compassion

"What does your inner child need to hear right now that no one ever told them? Write that message in your adult voice."

Purpose: Starts healing loop. You become your own source of safety and validation.

Step 5: Anchor a New Inner Identity

"Finish this sentence: 'My inner child is safe with me because I now…'"

Example:

"...honor their feelings, protect their light, and never force them to hide again."

Purpose: Ends with empowerment and responsibility. You become the protector, not the prisoner, of your past

PART III
UNMASKING YOUR ANCESTRY

If there is generational pain passed down,
mustn't there also be generational joy?
If there are family curses
that drop through time,
mustn't there also be family blessings
that do the same?"
- Jandy Nelson

CHAPTER 8

RELIVING THE ANCESTRAL LINEAGE

What You Will Unmask

In this chapter, I step into the sacred territory of ancestral memory and invite you to come with me. This is where the healing journey gets bigger than just you. If you've ever felt the weight of something that didn't start with you or the pull of patterns that seem older than your lifetime, this chapter will resonate. Through my experiences in Ghana and Australia, you'll be invited to consider that some of your wounds may be inherited, but so is your power. The wisdom, the pain, and the healing – it's all been encoded in your bloodline, waiting to be reclaimed.

We are not isolated beings, floating untethered through time. We are ripples in an ever-expanding ocean of existence, constantly influencing and being influenced by the past, present, and future. Every choice we make, every burden we carry, and every moment of healing we embrace reverberates across generations – both backward and forward. This is the essence of ancestral healing: the understanding that we are not just healing ourselves but also the unseen wounds of those who came before us, and paving the way for those who will follow.

We live in a culture that values accumulation. Whether it's material possessions, responsibilities, or emotional wounds, we often hold onto things in an attempt to create stability and security. But this sense of security is an illusion. Instead of safety, accumulation often brings stagnation and heaviness, an inherited burden passed down through generations.

Take, for example, a woman named Pita, who I met in Rwanda. Growing up, she watched her mother constantly struggle with financial insecurity, working multiple jobs and still feeling like it was never enough. Pita's grandmother had a similar story – having survived wartime scarcity, she hoarded food and money, always fearful that the past would repeat itself. This deep-rooted fear of lack was passed down like an invisible heirloom, shaping Pita's beliefs about survival. Even as an adult, with a stable job and resources, she still found herself gripped by anxiety, compulsively overworking and afraid to spend money, as if at any moment it could all disappear.

When Pita began her journey of ancestral healing, she realized she wasn't just carrying her own fears – she was carrying the fear of generations before her. Through deep introspection, therapy, and spiritual work, she started unmasking these inherited beliefs, consciously choosing to rewrite the narrative. In releasing her fear, she wasn't just freeing herself – she was honoring her mother and grandmother by allowing their struggles to transform into wisdom rather than continued suffering. And just as importantly, she was breaking the cycle for her own children, ensuring that they wouldn't inherit the same unspoken fears.

Unmasking Ancestral healing is not about blame; it's about acknowledgment and transformation. When we unmask these generational patterns – whether they are fears, traumas, or limiting beliefs – we don't just heal ourselves; we send healing waves backward and forward in time.

Think of it like a river. If pollution has been dumped into the water upstream, those downstream will suffer its effects. However, when someone makes the effort to cleanse the river at the source, those downstream will benefit, even if they never know the work that was done. In the same way, when we heal ourselves, we shift the energetic blueprint of our lineage, allowing those who came before us – and those who will come after – to find peace.

Consider my friend David. He grew up in a family where expressing emotions was seen as a weakness. His father rarely showed affection, and his grandfather was a stoic war veteran who had endured unspeakable hardships. David learned to suppress his emotions, believing that vulnerability was dangerous. As he got older, he struggled with relationships, unable to express his true feelings. It wasn't until he started therapy and engaged in inner work that he realized he was carrying generations of unspoken pain. By choosing to embrace vulnerability, to openly express love and break the cycle of emotional suppression, he wasn't just changing his own life – he was also healing the unseen wounds of his ancestors, who had never been given the space to feel and unmask.

Unmasking your ancestry is a sacred responsibility. To unmask is to acknowledge that we are part of a greater tapestry of existence. Our ancestors' experiences live within us, shaping our fears, desires, and choices. But we are not prisoners of the past – we are co-creators of our lineage's evolution. When we choose to heal, to break destructive cycles, and to embody love instead of fear, we are doing sacred work.

This healing ripples outward. It lifts the weight off our ancestors, many of whom never had the tools or the opportunity to process their pain. It liberates us in the present, allowing us to live with more freedom, joy, and authenticity. And it plants seeds for the future, ensuring that those who come after us inherit love and wisdom rather than unprocessed trauma.

Unmasking your Ancestry and healing is a gift, a bridge between worlds, a way to honor the past while creating a brighter future. We do not unmask to judge – we unmask to set ourselves free. And in that freedom, we find true connection, not only with ourselves but with the entire lineage of souls who have walked before and will walk after us.

THE UNMASKING TRIGGER
IN GHANA

My first time in West Africa hit me harder than I expected; nothing could have prepared me for visiting the enslavement dungeons. The moment I walked in, the air changed, becoming heavy with centuries of pain and loss. The small windows, high up on the walls, let in a cold light and kept any sense of freedom just out of reach. The stone floor told its own story through grooves carved by countless shackled feet pacing across it endlessly.

Everything about it, the musty smell, the cold stone walls with their desperate scratches, the worn steps leading down into darkness, all felt too real, too present. History stopped being something I'd read about and became something I could touch, smell, and feel in my bones. For a second, I wondered if I'd made a mistake bringing my kids, until I remembered that children their age had once been imprisoned here, torn from everything they knew.

I broke down. Not just quiet tears, but deep, gut-wrenching sobs that came from somewhere I didn't even know existed within me. It wasn't just my pain. It felt like generations of grief pouring out all at once. My children had never seen me cry like that or ever before. They reached for my hands, and that simple gesture of comfort only made me think of all the parents who'd stood in that very spot, holding their children for the last time.

That moment changed how I saw my family. Looking at my kids afterward, I felt the weight of both past and future on my shoulders. But it wasn't until months later, when my DNA results came back, that things started making sense. Even without knowing my ancestral ties, something about that land spoke to me.

The pain I'd felt in those dungeons wasn't just mine; it belonged to a long line of ancestors whose blood runs through my veins.

It taught me something about being vulnerable, too. My wife and kids had seen me cry before, but never like that. There was something powerful about letting myself feel everything in that moment, about not trying to be strong or composed.

The experience showed me that ancestral trauma isn't just a concept; it's real, living energy that flows through generations. But along with the pain, I found something else in those walls: an incredible will to survive. Standing in that sacred space, I felt both the depth of suffering and the height of human resilience.

I've been working on forgiveness since then. Not the easy kind that comes with a shrug, but the deep, complicated kind that forces you to face yourself and your history head-on. In doing so, I've opened up space for something bigger: for love and understanding at a level I didn't know I was capable of accessing.

That journey to Ghana didn't fix everything, but it cracked something open in me. Sometimes, healing starts with standing still in the hardest places, feeling everything, and then choosing how to carry that forward. It's about taking all that pain and turning it into something else – something that might help build a better world.

The masks we inherit – the ones that tell us to stay quiet, to feel less than, to carry pain in silence – are passed down through generations, and when we become aware of them, we need to make that decision so that it stops with us. Our children and the world deserve better.

AUSTRALIA

We traveled to Australia not long after visiting Ghana. It was like one of those tourist shows advertising an Outback farm. You know the type. Demonstrations of farm life, working with animals, fresh air, open spaces, that sort of thing. It seemed harmless enough at first. Then they started cracking the whip.

I'd never heard a whip crack in real life before. The sound hit me like a physical blow, and my whole body just … shut down. I went numb, frozen in place, as this wave of – I don't even know what to call it – swept through me. It wasn't exactly fear, at least not my own fear. It felt older than that, like some ancient memory buried in my bones. My muscles locked up, and I remember thinking, "What the hell is happening to me?"

The crazy thing is, I've never been hit with a whip, never even been close to one. But in that moment, that crack felt as if it had just struck my own back. I looked over at my wife, and I knew from her face that she had felt it too – this unexplainable, gut-level reaction to a sound that shouldn't have meant anything to us.

Then, the guy running the show asked if any kids wanted to come up and help with the animals or try the whip. My son's hand shot up, excited like any kid would be. Without even thinking, I grabbed him and pulled him close to me.

"No," I said, my voice shaking. "You're not going up there."

He looked up at me, confused.

I wasn't mad at him. How could I be? But something deep inside me couldn't bear the thought of him anywhere near that whip.

I'm still trying to make sense of what happened that day. That reaction, the numbness, the freezing up, the overwhelming dread, had felt like it belonged to someone else, like I was experiencing someone else's nightmare. Someone in my family line had heard that same sound and known it not as some farming tool but as an instrument of torture. Their terror lived on in me, passed down through generations like some genetic memory.

Sometimes I wonder: if I didn't know about my ancestry, would I have reacted the same way? If I hadn't known about the possible enslavement in my family's past, would that whip crack still have frozen me in place? I think it would have. That kind of trauma doesn't need your conscious mind to understand it – it lives in your body, in your cells, like an old scar you don't remember getting.

Unmasking isn't just about dealing with what you know happened; it's about facing what your body remembers, even when your mind can't explain it.

This stuff we inherit from our ancestors is heavy, of course, but it's also a source of strength. It reminds us that we come from survivors, from people who faced the unthinkable and kept going. That whip crack in Australia was a brutal reminder of what they endured, a legacy I didn't ask for but can't escape. But I'm learning that while I can't choose the pain I inherited, I can choose what to do with it. I can use it to build something better, something that honors their strength and helps heal the wounds they carried.

WELL OF FORGIVENESS

Something pulled me to Salaga, Nigeria, before I had even begun to know the details of my ancestry. My DNA results just said "Nigeria," but the urge to visit felt deeper than that, like something beyond my conscious mind was guiding me there.

I didn't know then that Salaga had been one of the major hubs throughout the transatlantic slave trade, home to one of West Africa's largest slave markets, and at the heart of where that market once stood is the Well of Attenuation. The name itself tells a story. *"Attenuation"* means to reduce in force or effect; it's a clinical word for something deeply sinister: the systematic and industrial breaking of human spirits.

The locals seemed hesitant to talk about it until I found an elder who knew its true purpose. He explained how the well served as both a practical and psychological tool in the slave trade. Captives were cleaned here before sale, but the well's primary purpose was far more insidious. Every person bound for slavery was forced to drink or bathe in its waters as part of a ritual meant to weaken their will and wash away their memories of home before the brutal journey across the Atlantic. The slavers believed, or at least used the belief, that the well's water had properties that could not only make people forget but also make them more compliant based on the rituals done to create those effects.

Standing there, the weight of history felt crushing.

The original stonework still visible around the well seemed to hold centuries of grief, as if the tears shed and drops of blood that fell there had seeped into the very ground. Though the water had long since disappeared, its presence felt alive, crying out for all those whose spirits were meant to be broken here.

A part of my identity died but was simultaneously reborn in seeing that well. I can't say for certain that someone from my direct bloodline was thrown into it, but I know I was meant to be there. There was a knowing in my bones – that ancestral memory lives in the body – and I knew that my people had come through here. The Igbo people. So when I visit places like Ghana, Nigeria, or Toga lands soaked in suffering, it's never just history. It's sacred ground.

What came up in Salaga wasn't just emotion; there was a moment of synchronicity. I needed to be there. To witness. To release. To close a loop that had been left open somewhere along my lineage, or perhaps even beyond it.

Because when I go to these places, I don't go only as myself. I go as a vessel, holding space for my ancestors, for my descendants, and for humanity. I'm an ambassador of healing. That's what resonates deeply for me. That's the calling I live by.

Some of the places I've ended up in weren't even planned. I was guided, pulled by something greater than logic. And just by standing there, I experience transformation. In healing myself, I help to heal the lineage.

That has led me to discover the truth that not all ancestors are linked by blood. We're linked through frequency. Some people in your family tree may not be your ancestors in spirit, and some who aren't in your tree at all, absolutely are. We're bound by energy, resonance, and memories.

So when I walked into that space, I felt like I wasn't just walking for me. I was walking for those who couldn't. For those who were made to forget. In that space, transformation found me. The spark within those captives did not die. It was passed down, buried deep in the cells, waiting to be reawakened. That spark called me there. And when I poured libations, offered prayers, and performed rituals of cleansing and release, I wasn't just honoring the past; I was helping to actively shift its echo in the present.

Across the Slave Coast – in Ghana, Togo, Benin, Nigeria, the Ivory Coast – there are wells like this. Wells of forgetting. Places where enslaved people were ritually stripped of memory and will. The Well of Memory Loss in Badagry. The Assin Manso Slave River in Ghana. The Tree of Oblivion in Whydah. These weren't isolated practices. They were coordinated efforts to dehumanise swathes of people.

But what was meant to erase us only left trails, energetic fingerprints, for us to follow back. Even though the water has now been gone for centuries, it still holds memories.. It carries the essence of what was done there. It affects our frequency.

Just like in electronics, where you reduce voltage to reduce power, these rituals were meant to reduce our spiritual voltage. And now, our task is to reclaim it, to amplify, to remember who we truly are: unfiltered, uncolonised, unbroken.

Forgiveness came to me in that space not to excuse what was done, but to break the generational chains. Forgiveness for the tormentors. Forgiveness for the silence. Forgiveness even for the parts of myself that still carried that inherited pain.

It's a strange paradox: only by walking into the darkest places can we begin to reclaim our light. The Well of Attenuation was designed to weaken spirits. But standing there, reclaiming the narrative, I felt stronger than ever. That's the triumph. That's the healing. Turning a place of pain into a portal of power.

What You Have Unmasked

Reaching the end of this chapter, you have now opened the door to your lineage – not just to understand it but to transform it. I've re-walked the paths of my ancestors, and you've been prompted to begin noticing yours. You've likely felt a stirring, a sense that your story is part of something much older and more sacred. You've started the work of healing backward, so you and future generations can walk forward freer.

CHAPTER 9

OVERCOMING THE ANCESTRAL BURDEN

What You Will Unmask

In this chapter, I confront a powerful truth: not all of what I carry is mine. You'll be invited to recognize how inherited fears, beliefs, and behavioral patterns can silently run your life – until you name them. If you've ever wondered why you repeat patterns even after doing "the work" or feel haunted by weight you can't explain, this chapter will hit home. You'll begin to understand how ancestral burdens are passed down through story, silence, and even biology, and that you hold the authority to break the chain.

Our family history shapes us more deeply than we realize. The behaviors and emotional patterns we inherit aren't random – they're deeply rooted connections passed down through generations. Understanding these inherited influences requires looking at both scientific and emotional perspectives.

Modern science, particularly epigenetics, now confirms what traditional wisdom has long understood. Our experiences can modify how our genes function, creating lasting impacts that can be passed down through families.

These changes don't alter our genetic code, but they do influence how our genes express themselves, affecting our behaviors, emotions, and even our physical health.

When family patterns go unaddressed, destructive patterns continue. Issues like addiction, financial struggles, and unresolved grief repeat themselves until someone consciously decides to break the cycle. Those patterns are often closely linked to the emotional masks we learn to wear during childhood, creating a complex web of inherited conditioning.

Emotional inheritance runs deep. The fears, limiting beliefs, and survival strategies of our ancestors live on in us. For instance, historical struggles for survival can create a persistent fear of loss that continues long after the original circumstances have changed. These fears become embedded in family dynamics, subtly guiding how generations navigate their lives.

This inheritance isn't just metaphorical – it's physically carried within us. Scientific research and ancestral wisdom both suggest that unresolved emotions can be transmitted across generations. Even before birth, the emotional experiences of previous generations can subtly influence future family members. For example, in Jamaica, it was common for parents who couldn't care for all their children to send some to live with relatives. While done out of necessity, that practice often created deep feelings of rejection and abandonment. Those emotions would then unconsciously pass from one generation to the next, creating a cycle of emotional pain.

Recognizing inherited patterns is the first step to unmasking. When we work to understand and transform our family's emotional legacy, we don't just change our own lives – we alter the trajectory for future generations.

ANCESTRY IS NOT DESTINY

Inherited patterns are universal, existing across different cultures and societies. Beyond obvious historical traumas, more subtle forms of generational influence continue to shape our experiences. In many societies, systemic inequities and historical oppression create lasting impacts that ripple through families. Healing begins with honest acknowledgment and facing the reality of our past in its entirety while not minimizing or avoiding difficult truths. We must be willing to look directly at what has been passed down, identify patterns, and understand their impact.

There were once two brothers, both raised by the same criminal father, who took dramatically different paths in life. One followed his father's criminal lifestyle, while the other became a respected community member. When asked how they became who they were, both gave the same response: "With a father like that, what else could I have been?"

This story reveals that trauma and adversity don't determine a single outcome. The outcome is shaped by how individuals process and respond to what they receive. Our past doesn't define our destiny; we have the power to choose our path. While it is very useful to know of the hardships that have occurred, we cannot let them define our future paths.

Even within a single family, individuals can process inherited influences differently. My own siblings and I, raised under the same roof, have carved unique paths shaped by our shared ancestral background but processed in distinct ways. This is true even for my extended family.

I remember when my grandmother would buy chicken; she would purchase half a bird and carefully divide it to ensure everyone ate.

When I suggested buying a whole chicken as being more economical, she explained, "I can only spend what I have, and I make it stretch."

Years later, seeing my aunt cook a whole chicken during Christmas revealed a different perspective – one of abundance and celebration. This wasn't just about food but about recognizing our ancestors' ingenuity while expanding what's possible.

These inherited patterns of thinking about money, success, and possibility are part of our family legacy. I realized that we can consciously choose which parts of this legacy to preserve and which to transform. Our ancestors gave us survival; we can now create opportunities for thriving.

Ancestral trauma isn't just about wounds; it also carries unexpected strengths. Take the Black community's experience, for example. Despite immense suffering, forced separations created powerful traditions of resilience and unity. Family reunions became more than gatherings; they were sacred spaces of reconnection, storytelling, and reclaiming bonds that history tried to sever.

Our Ancestral Masks contain both pain and strength, loss and resilience, trauma and triumph. Unmasking them isn't about dwelling on hardship, placing blame, or harboring resentment, but about reclaiming the wisdom and power that have carried our families forward.

TUNING IN TO THE
ANCESTRAL WAVELENGTHS

"I am the dream of my ancestors.
I am their voice, their healing, and their liberation.
As I heal, they rise.
As I rise, so does my lineage."
–Ike Anderson

Something that I feel I need to address is what I mean when I say ancestors.

When I talk about ancestors, I'm really talking about a two-way energy connection that goes beyond blood relations. Think of it like a spiritual radio signal; you can connect with energies that match your own frequency, whether they're from your bloodline or your spiritual tribe. And just as a radio needs to be tuned to the right frequency to get a clear signal (96.5 FM vs. AM), we need to be aligned to connect with specific ancestral energies. The connections are always available, but the quality depends on the state of our own energy.

These ancestral energies can be guides, our protectors, or even serve as our teachers. However, it's important to understand that they operate on an exchange principle – some require offerings or energy, such as an ancestral altar to provide guidance in return. That isn't negative; it's just how certain relationships work on the energetic level. With that said, don't give away your power, as self-sovereignty is paramount.

Our own energy level directly affects which ancestral energies we attract. If we're feeling low, we might connect with heavier energies. When we're vibrating higher, we attract more elevated guidance. It's like tuning that radio dial – different frequencies bring in different stations.

The key isn't to always maintain high energy but to stay aware of where your energy is at any given moment. When you're in a lower state, don't try to escape it. Instead, ask yourself: "What can I learn here? Should I stay with this feeling or shift my energy?" Being present and conscious of your energy state, whether high or low, gives you control over these ancestral connections.

I learned this through experience. Initially, I tried to avoid lower energies altogether, but that didn't work. True power comes from being aware and present, regardless of your energy state, understanding that you always have a choice in how you engage with your ancestral connections.

For me, ancestral healing is more than just a concept. It has been a living, breathing, soul-deep journey of remembrance and return. Over the years, ancestral connection has become one of the most vital parts of my unmasking. The deeper I went within, the more I could feel the pull of an energetic beckoning from beyond time. It was calling me to remember, to return, and to restore balance in places my ancestors once walked.

That call led me and my family to Scotland. It wasn't just a trip. It was a pilgrimage, a sacred journey guided by something older than memory. I began to realize that some of us are spiritually assigned to close energetic loops in the places where our bloodlines originated. For many, ancestral healing may happen in dreamwork, rituals, or internal journeys, but for others, it requires movement, a physical return to the land that once held the stories, joys, and pain of our lineage.

As we boarded the plane, I didn't know exactly what I would find. I only knew this: my soul had business there. And not just for me – for my ancestors, my children, and for humanity at large.

Arriving in Glasgow, I felt an inexplicable peace settle into my bones. It was as if something ancient within me exhaled for the first time. Though I had never been to Scotland before, everything felt strangely familiar – like a homecoming of the soul.

As we journeyed through the Highlands, I could feel the residue of old stories, not just historical ones, but spiritual imprints left in the land. There was a cathartic release, a sacred unburdening, as if I was carrying something on behalf of generations before me. A weight I didn't know I had been carrying began to lift. It was not sadness or pain, but a deep soul-knowing: You are not separate. You are the continuation.

In some cases, ancestral healing must be embodied, and travel becomes the sacred container for that embodiment. When our physical body meets ancestral ground, something activates. Our DNA remembers. Our spirit stirs. And if we are willing to listen, to feel, and to unmask the silent burdens we carry, we can heal not only ourselves but also those who came before us – and those who will come after.

We are often called to specific places because our frequency is ready to align with the ancestral wavelength that lives there. We become vessels of reconciliation. Through our presence, we bless what was never acknowledged, forgive what was never apologized for, and liberate those who could not liberate themselves.

In doing so, we give the future permission to live freely, unbound by the emotional echoes of the past.

In my case, the history is complex. DNA testing revealed that I am 18% European: my ancestors from the British Isles made their way to Jamaica in the 1700s and 1800s during colonization. Some may have come in pursuit of opportunity; others may have caused harm. My Jamaican bloodline holds both the oppressed and the oppressor.

Most Jamaicans – over 85% – carry Scottish surnames. Mine are no exception: Farquharson and Anderson. Both are deeply rooted in Scottish soil.

Standing on that same soil generations later, I didn't come with blame. I came with intention. I came to honor the benevolent, forgive the harmful, and reconcile the pain and power that made my very existence possible.

Because here's the truth: I wouldn't be here if history had unfolded any other way.

This is the paradox of ancestral healing. We acknowledge the trauma while also honoring the survival. We unmask the inherited burdens, not to dwell in pain, but to liberate the energy trapped in silence, shame, and suppression. This is what I experienced – a soul retrieval for my lineage.

We often think of healing as something we do for ourselves. But healing ripples in both directions: backward through the timelines of our ancestors and forward into the lives of those yet to be born. When we choose healing, we become the link that breaks the chain.

We become what our ancestors dreamed of but never saw.

We become the ones who speak when they could not, dance when they were forbidden, love when they were shamed, and live when they were only surviving.

At its core, this journey is not just about heritage. It's about humanity. The unmasking of our ancestral layers leads us to a deeper truth: we are all connected. Without love and mutual respect, the cycles of division, hate, and suppression continue. But through healing, we begin to remember that we are one body of humanity-and we carry the power to shift collective consciousness by first shifting within.

This journey changed me. It helped me remember my sacred responsibility to unmask not only for myself but for those who came before me and those who will come after. It revealed to me that healing is not passive; it is a conscious, sometimes uncomfortable, always powerful return to wholeness.

And now, as we continue to journey across the world as a family, we do so with intention – to honor, to heal, and to remember. This is the unmasking effect in motion. The remembrance that history is not just behind us; it's within us. And we are here now, rewriting it in love.

What You Have Unmasked

I've learned that ancestry is not destiny. And so have you. Have you begun to reclaim your personal power from generations past – not in rejection, but with reverence? You now carry the awareness that you can be the turning point, the healing link, the one who transforms legacy into liberation. This chapter gave you permission to stop carrying what was never yours to hold.

CHAPTER 10

EPIGENETICS: THE SCIENCE BEHIND ANCESTRAL UNMASKING

What You Will Unmask

In this chapter, I bring the fragmented pieces of my journey into alignment. You've been walking through this process with me – you've seen the chaos, the ancestry, the internal programming, the spiritual whispers – all of it. Now, I'm stepping into the space where everything comes together in conscious embodiment.

You'll walk with me through the integration of Human Design, ancestral healing, epigenetic patterns, and soul purpose. But more than anything, you'll witness what it means to live liberated-not as a concept, but as a daily vibration.

This isn't about learning another theory. This is about breathing as the truth of who you are-
no longer hiding from your own greatness.

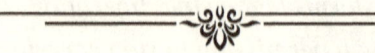

In recent decades, the field of epigenetics has provided scientific evidence that bridges the gap between ancient wisdom and modern understanding. For centuries, cultures worldwide have recognised the influence of ancestors on our lives, attributing traits, strengths, and struggles to those who came before us. But epigenetics now offers a biological explanation for how this influence manifests, affirming that ancestral healing is not just a spiritual journey but also a physiological process.

At its core, epigenetics studies how environmental factors can influence the way our genes are expressed without altering the DNA sequence itself. While genes provide the blueprint for our biology, epigenetic mechanisms act as "switches," determining which parts of that blueprint are activated or silenced. These switches are influenced by life experiences: stress, trauma, diet, and even emotional states. What is remarkable is that these epigenetic modifications can be passed down through generations.

One of the most compelling examples of epigenetics in action is how trauma leaves biological marks that can be seen in future generations. Research on survivors of highly traumatic events has shown that their descendants often exhibit heightened stress responses, despite not experiencing the original trauma themselves. Similarly, studies on populations affected by famine reveal that the children and grandchildren of those who endured starvation have an increased likelihood of developing metabolic disorders, even when raised in abundance.

This inheritance is not metaphorical; it's encoded in the very systems that regulate our biology. Trauma doesn't just affect the individual who experiences it; it reverberates through their lineage. This understanding challenges the idea that we are born as blank slates, unmarked by history. Instead, it paints a picture of intergenerational connection, where the pain, resilience, and survival strategies of our ancestors are engraved into our biology.

RITUALS AT THE CELLULAR LEVEL

In many cultures throughout history, rituals have played a central role in ancestral connection and healing, acting as a bridge between the physical and the spiritual. From the importance of a name in Celtic history to the spiritualism of Native Americans to the concept of reincarnation in Hinduism, Buddhism, and Jainism, these practices of memory and influence align closely with the principles of epigenetics. While the hard science focuses on biological changes, rituals often focus on symbolic and emotional shifts, which in turn influence our biological state.

For example, when I visited the enslavement dungeons in Ghana, the experience was profoundly visceral. It wasn't just emotional; it felt cellular. Later, during cleansing rituals performed by local elders, I realized how intentional acts can release not only the energy of the past but also the biological imprints tied to it.

Science supports that connection. When we engage in rituals of acknowledgment and release, we activate processes in the brain and body that reduce stress, regulate emotions, and foster healing. Those processes have measurable effects on gene expression, affirming that what we do on a symbolic level also impacts our biology.

What epigenetics shows us is that cycles of trauma and dysfunction aren't inevitable; awareness is the first step in breaking those cycles. When we understand that some of our struggles are inherited, it shifts the narrative from one of blame to one of empowerment. Instead of asking, "What's wrong with me?" we begin to ask, "What story am I carrying, and how can I transform it?"

For example, in my journey, as I strengthened my awareness, I came to understand how ancestral patterns of scarcity influenced my relationship with finances and abundance. Growing up, there was an underlying sense of survival, of always needing to work harder, be smarter, and prepare for the worst. Perhaps this was something rooted in watching how my grandmother made the most out of having so little. But as I unmasked those patterns, I began to shift them, replacing them with beliefs and practices rooted in trust, alignment, and purpose.

That shift wasn't just theoretical; it was also physiological. Practices like breathwork and grounding helped me calm my nervous system, reducing the stress response that had been passed down through my lineage. Over time, I felt the ripple effects of this healing not only in myself but also in my family.

HOPE UNDERSCORES EPIGENETICS

Epigenetics doesn't only explain how trauma is inherited. For those on the journey of ancestral healing, the findings offer clarity and hope. They suggest that the heaviness we sometimes carry – the anxiety, the fear, the sense of disconnection – may not entirely belong to us. Instead, those feelings could be echoes of experiences lived by those who came before us, imprinted on our genetic fabric as a call to address what remains unresolved. Epigenetics also shows us that change is possible, not just for ourselves but for those who came before us and those who will follow. Every act of healing, no matter how small, is a step toward rewriting the biological and energy story of our lineage.

By embracing ancestral healing through the lens of epigenetics, we honor the scientific truth that we are shaped by our past while reclaiming the spiritual truth that we are also the authors of our own futures. This dual awareness is what makes the journey of unmasking so profound.

While epigenetics shows us how trauma is transmitted, it also reveals the profound potential for healing. Just as negative experiences can imprint on our genes, positive changes can shift those imprints. Studies on mindfulness practices, healthy diets, and stress-reduction techniques have demonstrated their ability to alter gene expression, sometimes within weeks. These shifts aren't just temporary; they have the potential to be passed onto future generations.

Unmasking Ancestral healing, therefore, is where science aligns with spirituality. It becomes a process of not only addressing the past but also consciously shaping the future. When we engage in practices like meditation, breathwork, and rituals of release, we aren't just healing our own lives; we're creating new patterns that our descendants will inherit.

What You Have Unmasked

In this chapter, you've been handed the keys to make your personal liberation more than a moment –
it becomes a rhythm.
You've seen how I blended science, spirituality, and identity work into something usable. Something real.
I showed you how I got back in my body, back into alignment, and stopped betraying myself for the sake of survival.
You've been offered not only frameworks but an invitation: to live your integration out loud, to stop code-switching between your inner self and outer image. You now understand that embodiment is not the end. It's the beginning of contribution. Of service. Of being a signal for others who are ready to rise.

114

CHAPTER 11
UNMASKING THE ANCESTRAL MASK

What You Will Unmask

This chapter brings a moment where I had to decide: would I show up masked, polished, performing... or would I let my truth speak without a filter? Everything I've talked about in this book – ancestral patterns, childhood pain, societal roles – it all surfaced in one interaction.

I'm telling you this story because I know you've had those moments, too. The ones where your body remembers the old role, and you feel that familiar pull to shrink. My hope is that as you read this, you'll start to recognize your own power to choose differently-not by force, but by awareness. You'll see that the moment you choose truth over performance, your entire path begins to shift.

Clearing the past doesn't mean erasing it. As I've discussed, it's about recognizing the lessons, integrating them into the present, and using them to move forward purposefully. Every step becomes conscious, aware, and deeply connected. This is how the burdens of the past are reborn.

"What was meant for your demise,
I use for your good."
—Genesis 50:20

I think this truly summarizes the position we are in when we decide to remove Ancestral Masks that no longer serve us. We can choose to reframe or remove something that was created by our ancestors for survival, to strengthen their resilience in the hardship that now limits us.

It is a concept that also occurs in various places and cultures, and even in religion. For example, in Genesis 50:20, this quote is replicated: "As for you, you meant evil against me, but God meant it for good in order to bring about this present result, to keep many people alive." It is the same idea of reframing challenge, difficulty, and even trauma from the perspective of faith.

It's a concept that, no matter how it is presented, deeply resonates with ancestral unmasking. While it's impossible to deny the atrocities and struggles experienced by previous generations, those experiences can also be sources of profound empowerment and growth for us today. Reclaiming the sacrifices of our ancestors allows us to transform inherited imprints into something that serves us rather than limits us.

However, we need to recognize that even the language we use when talking about this unmasking matters. Words carry energy, and choosing the right ones is vital in shaping how we approach and understand this process. Take the word "wound," for example. When we think of a wound, it often conjures up images of something visible, a gaping hole, a physical injury. Ancestral experiences aren't visible; they exist in our energy, in our patterns, in the things passed down to us that we don't consciously recognize.

This is where reframing becomes critical. What if we thought of these "wounds" not as damage but as events or imprints? By removing the emotional charge while still honoring the depth of the experience, we can create a healthier relationship with our past.

That doesn't dismiss the pain or ignore the reality of what happened; it's about acknowledging it in a way that empowers us to move forward.

The question then becomes: "Do you have to feel the pain fully to truly acknowledge it?" The answer isn't simple. There's the evolved, conscious perspective, where we see the events of the past as lessons, detached from their emotional weight. And then there's the deeply human, three-dimensional experience, where pain demands to be felt before it can be released. Both perspectives have their place, and navigating between them is part of each individual journey.

Ancestral unmasking is not a straightforward process, and it can feel deeply personal and layered. There's a duality to it: the balance between honoring the struggles of the past and choosing to live beyond them. It requires us to step back and ask questions that challenge our inherited beliefs:

- Is this my truth?

- Does this story serve me?

- What strength can I draw from my ancestors while releasing what no longer aligns with me?

At its core, unmasking ancestral influences is about reclaiming agency. It's about understanding that the imprints we carry, be they energy, emotional, or cultural, don't define us. They inform us, yes, but we have the power to choose what we carry forward. It's not about erasing the past but about transforming its impact into something that empowers us in the present.

This journey is deeply healing, not just for ourselves but for the generations to come. When we confront and release the burdens passed down to us, we interrupt the cycle. We create space for ourselves to flourish, not only within ourselves but also in the legacy we leave behind.

UNMASKING AND RECLAIMING YOUR ANCESTRY

Healing ancestral wounds is a journey of both acknowledgment and transformation. The past influences our present in ways we may not realize, but by confronting inherited pain, we open the door to strength, resilience, and wholeness. Here are some of the steps I took that may help you navigate the process along your journey.

1. Recognize the Ancestral Masks You Carry

The first step is awareness. The emotional burdens, beliefs, and patterns you carry may not have started with you; they could be echoes of generations before you. These inherited influences often operate beneath the surface, subtly shaping how you see yourself, how you move through the world, and even how you respond to challenges.

Ask yourself:

- What struggles, fears, or limiting beliefs seem to repeat in my family?

- Are there cultural or familial expectations that don't align with who I truly am?

- Do I feel a weight that I can't fully explain, as if something beyond my own experiences is influencing me?

- Is there something specific that affects the women or men in my family?

By recognizing these patterns, you begin the process of bringing them into conscious awareness, loosening their hold over you.

2. Trace the Origins of Your Inherited Patterns

Understanding where these ancestral imprints come from allows you to begin healing them. Generational wounds don't appear out of nowhere; they are often shaped by historical traumas, societal oppression, cultural upheavals, or personal family hardships that have been unconsciously passed down.

Reflect on the stories that your family has passed down. What is the narrative you carry with you, and from that narrative, do you carry an unexplained sense of fear, guilt, or lack?

Remember, this is not about blaming the past but about understanding its imprint on *your* present.

3. Acknowledge Generational Trauma and Strength

Just as trauma can be inherited, so can resilience. The same bloodline that carries wounds also carries wisdom, perseverance, and deep-rooted strength. Recognizing both sides of your ancestry allows for a more balanced perspective. Don't only consider what aspects of your ancestors' experience have limited you, but also what strengths, emotional, creative, or spiritual, have been passed down through your lineage.

By doing this, you honor not just the pain of your ancestors but also the gifts they left behind. You are a product of their sacrifices, their courage, and their determination to keep going.

4. Release and Reframe the Narrative

Healing doesn't mean forgetting – it means choosing how the past will shape you moving forward. You are not bound to repeat the same cycles; you have the power to shift your story.

Ask yourself:

- What inherited burdens am I ready to let go of?

- How can I honor my ancestors while living in alignment with my own truth?

- What new beliefs do I want to cultivate for future generations?

Reframing means transforming inherited pain into a source of wisdom. It means taking what was meant to limit you and using it to fuel your growth.

5. Engage in Ancestral Healing Practices

Ancestral healing is both symbolic and tangible. Small, intentional actions can create lasting change, shifting not just your experience but the energy of your lineage.

Learn about your family's history and share it. Trace your ancestry and see how you can honor ancestors in your life – whether that's lighting a candle, preparing a meal, or offering a prayer for their peace and guidance. Strengthen your connection to the past so that you can honor every part of what has brought you to this point.

But also take the time to work on healing yourself. The body remembers what the mind forgets, so engage in practices like breathwork and meditation to release stored trauma and embrace forgiveness.

Forgiveness is key because we don't want to erase the past; we want to free ourselves from its hold. Forgiveness is a tool of liberation, allowing you to unburden yourself from resentment and inherited pain.

6. Choose What You Carry Forward

You have the power to decide what serves you and what does not. Your lineage is a toolbox. You can pick up the tools that empower you and leave behind the ones that no longer align with your growth.

Ask yourself:

- Which traditions, beliefs, or stories empower me?

- What am I consciously choosing to pass on?

- How can I embody both my history and my individuality?

Healing is about discernment, about knowing that you are both a continuation of your lineage and an individual with the right to shape your own destiny.

UNMASKING THE WISDOM
OF OUR ANCESTORS

The journey of ancestral unmasking is never truly complete. It's a living, breathing process that pulses with the same energy that has carried our lineage through generations of challenge and triumph. So take this as your invitation to look deeper and listen more carefully to the whispers of those who came before us.

Our ancestors didn't just survive; they created intricate webs of resilience, pain, and hope that we now hold within our very cells. Epigenetics has shown us that these stories are living energies; they shape our present and future. We are not passive recipients of this inheritance. We are active creators, capable of transforming what was once a burden into a source of unprecedented strength.

Each family carries its own unique blueprint, a pattern copied over and over with each passing generation. Some patterns emerge as protective mechanisms, carefully crafted by those who came before us to navigate impossible circumstances; others show up as subtle limitations, quietly guiding our choices.

The beauty of this work lies in our ability to see these patterns with compassion, to understand their origins, and to consciously choose which threads we'll continue to weave. Some of those original patterns still serve us, but for the ones that no longer serve us, we need to remove those masks.

Remember, unmasking is not about reaching a state of perfection; that is an impossible task. It's about presence and awareness; it's about standing in the full complexity of our lineage, the wounds and the victories, and knowing what will not only serve us but also serve future generations as we carry on. We are both the guardians of our family's legacy and the architects of its future.

When we approach our ancestral journey with curiosity instead of judgment, we open ourselves to a profound form of healing. We can begin to see that the pain carried through generations is not a curse, but a call: a call to understand, to transform, to liberate both ourselves and those who will come after us.

The masks are falling. Your true story is emerging, not as a rejection of the past but as its most powerful continuation.

What You Have Unmasked

*You've now seen what it looks like when this work
walks into a real room. When I dropped the mask
and chose truth, something clicked into place –
not just for me but for how I move through the world.
And now, you've got a mirror. Maybe this helped you name the
part of you that still softens your truth for comfort. Maybe it
gave you permission to stop explaining your becoming to
people who never saw your becoming in the first place.
Either way, this is your moment
to stop negotiating with your freedom.*

PERSONAL LIBERATION BLUEPRINT – PART III

We carry the burdens, beliefs, and behaviors of our ancestors – many of which are not our own. Healing begins with remembrance, reverence, and conscious release. This moment turns ancestral trauma into **ancestral partnership**. It gives you the power to reframe your bloodline-not just grieve it. This is leadership through lineage.

Step 1: Name the Inherited Patterns

What beliefs, fears, or emotional responses have you carried that may not have started with you? Where in your life do you feel like you're reenacting someone else's story?

Purpose: Connects personal struggle to ancestral lineage-externalizes shame and creates space for compassion.

Step 2: Identify the Wound's Source

What is one story, myth, or memory-told or untold-that lives in your family line and still echoes in your choices?

Purpose: Reclaims context. Gives the pain roots and meaning.

Step 3: Honor the Survival That Came Before You

What did your ancestors have to endure or believe in order for you to be alive today? What did they give up so you could exist?

Purpose: Alchemizes resentment into reverence. Unlocks gratitude and ancestral pride.

Step 4: Choose What You Will Break and What You Will Keep

Which part of your ancestral story is asking to be broken-and which part do you choose to carry forward with honor?

Purpose: Empowers sovereignty. Not all lineage is poison-some is power.

Step 5: Create Your Lineage Liberation Prayer

Write a short invocation that declares your freedom from inherited pain *and* your commitment to carrying the gifts of your lineage with love.

Example:

"I break the chains that do not serve me. I carry forward the wisdom, strength, and soul of my people. I am the first and the future."

Purpose: Ceremony through words. You become the healer, not the haunted.

PART IV
UNMASKING SOCIETAL INFLUENCES

"Never forget that only dead fish swim with the stream."
– Malcolm Muggeridge

CHAPTER 12
INFLUENCES ALL AROUND US

What You Will Unmask

This chapter is where the lens shifts from inward to outward. I started noticing how the world around me – media, culture, religion, education – had shaped how I saw myself long before I ever got the chance to define who I was. Maybe you've felt that, too. Like the choices you make don't always feel like yours.

Here, I pull back the curtain on those external influences – not to blame them, but to reclaim my authority. If you've ever wondered why certain beliefs feel heavy, certain paths feel expected, or certain masks feel impossible to remove ... this chapter might help you see what isn't really yours to carry. This is about remembering your sovereignty in a world that trained you to forget it.

Societal masks are the expectations and roles imposed on us by our community, family, and culture. They tell us who we need to be, often at the expense of who we truly are.

From an early age, most of us are handed a blueprint for life: go to school, get a good career, secure a stable job, and follow a path that society deems successful. While these goals may offer structure and security, they can also become a framework of limitations. If we deviate from them, we're made to feel like we've failed.

To avoid that feeling of "being a failure," we put on more masks that lead us to live lives dictated by external expectations rather than internal passions.

For instance, consider a naturally gifted creative pushed to attend law school or train as a doctor. They might excel in their work, earning accolades and fulfilling societal standards, but deep down, they remain unfulfilled. The mask they've worn to fit in with societal norms has obscured their true, unique gifts.

The concept of societal masks goes deeper than just career choices. It's about how we're conditioned to act, think, and present ourselves in ways that align with what others expect of us, often suppressing our individuality in the process.

A MOMENT OF REALIZATION

It was a Friday afternoon, and I had taken a break from work to have lunch with one of my daughters at her school. It was one of those simple moments you look forward to as a parent, a chance to connect and step into their world. What I witnessed in that brief time would change the course of our lives.

As I walked through the halls, I noticed a bright yellow line painted on the floor of the walkway. At first, it seemed insignificant; it was just part of the everyday structure of a school. But then I saw how the children moved around it. They weren't allowed to step on it. Every single one of them had to stay in a perfectly straight line, walking single file toward the cafeteria.

I stood there, watching in silence, and something inside me began to stir. Every child obediently followed the rule, heads down, steps carefully placed to avoid crossing the line. They moved like robots, devoid of energy or individuality. That's when I spotted my daughter among them.

She was doing exactly what the other children were doing, staying in line, walking with quiet compliance. My free-spirited, creative, vibrant daughter was now just another figure in the line, blending in, following the rules without question.

My heart sank.

I couldn't help but think, "No, this isn't right. This isn't who she is. This isn't who we are."

At that moment, the sight of her in that line triggered something deep within me. I flashed back to my own childhood. I've always been the kind of person who, as a kid, would've jumped on that yellow line.

I would've danced on it, stomped on it, and dared someone to tell me otherwise. Rules like that felt like a cage to me, a stifling force that sought to contain who I was. And yet, there I was, watching my child being molded into the very thing I'd spent so much of my life resisting.

That moment brought back so many memories of my own childhood, the rigid routines and rules I had to follow growing up. I couldn't leave the house without my clothes pressed to perfection, starched so stiff they could stand up on their own. It wasn't just expected; it was demanded.

I remember mornings at school when we'd line up for inspection. They'd check our shoes to make sure they were spotless, our uniforms crisp, and our haircuts fresh. If you didn't meet the standard, you'd face the consequences. There was no room for individuality, no space for deviation. Every detail was scrutinized, and falling short wasn't an option.

I carried that conditioning with me for years, not even questioning it. It wasn't until much later in life that I saw it for what it was: an invisible framework of expectations. It was a system that valued appearances over authenticity. It made me realize that the same rigidity I had endured as a child was being passed down to her, just wrapped in a different package.

Then, it hit me like a tidal wave: I was complicit. I had unknowingly become part of the system – the rules, the conformity, the quiet obedience – that was shaping her.

That evening, I couldn't keep the thoughts to myself. I spoke to my wife, pouring out everything I felt. "Honey," I said, "We have to make some changes. I can't do this. We're creating robots, and I feel like we're in a cage ourselves."

She listened to everything I had to say, to every thought and complaint, no matter how coherent they were. Her free-spirited nature reflected my own. She saw it, too. We both knew that something had to change for our children and for our family. It was a turning point. It was the moment we decided to break free and try something *radical*.

We questioned everything: the routines, the structure of our lives, even the 5,000-square-foot home that we had worked so hard to build. It was comfortable and stable, but it was also a cage, filled with the same societal expectations and pressures we wanted to escape.

We made the leap and decided to leave behind the life we knew and embark on a journey. It wasn't just a physical journey but a journey of unlearning. We wanted to strip away the layers of societal influence that had shaped us, to step outside of the expectations and rediscover what it meant to live freely.

Travel became our new way of life. With every new place we visited, we peeled back a layer of the masks we had been wearing. We began to see the world, and ourselves, differently.

Through this process, I began to understand that societal influence isn't always overt. It doesn't always announce itself loudly. Often, it's subtle, woven into the fabric of daily life, from the way children are taught to line up at school to the unspoken expectations of adulthood. It shapes how we think, how we act, and how we raise our children, often without us even realizing it.

Unmasking societal influence forces us to ask whether the life we are living is truly our own or merely a product of the systems we've been taught to follow. It's about giving ourselves and our children the freedom to step off the yellow line, to dance on it if they choose, and to create lives that are authentic and unbound by the expectations of others.

This isn't an easy process. It requires courage, vulnerability, and a willingness to let go of what feels safe. But it's worth it.

For me, that moment in the school hallway was a gift. It was a wake-up call, a chance to course-correct before it was too late. It reminded me of who I am and who I want my children to be. It was about reclaiming my own sense of freedom and giving that same gift to my children. It was about showing them that life doesn't have to be lived in a straight line. It can be messy, creative, and full of surprises.

RECONSIDERING EVERYTHING

What began as a simple realization during that visit to the school cafeteria was just the tip of the iceberg. It spiraled into a much deeper, more existential reconsideration of the world around me. The more I thought about it, the more I saw how much of my life, how much of *our* lives, is shaped by unseen societal influences.

Take religion, for example. It's one of the clearest and most pervasive influences on our beliefs and behaviors. It tells us what's right and wrong, how to live, and what to aspire to ... but who decides what's "right"? How much of what we believe is truly ours, and how much of it is inherited, passed down unquestioned through generations?

Another powerful example is the way society defines masculinity and femininity. We're told how to act, what roles we should play, and what it means to be a "man" or a "woman." These messages shape us in significant ways, influencing our relationships, careers, and even how we see ourselves. They're so embedded in our culture that they can feel like the truth, even when they might not align with who we really are.

When you have that first realization, when you ask those first questions, it sets off a chain reaction of questions that can take us to some uncomfortable places. It pushes us into the "deep, dark night of the soul," which I discussed in the preceding parts of this book.

During this time, we question *everything* – not just our roles as a parent, a friend, a partner ... but as a human being. We start to wonder: Who are we *really?* What do we *truly* believe? Are the thoughts and ideas we carry even *ours*, or are they a product of the world we grew up in?

At one point, I remember thinking about something as simple as the color red. Who decided it was red? What does "red" even mean?

We're taught these things so early that we accept them as fact, but what if they're not? This line of questioning didn't stop at colors; it extended to my personality, my behaviors, and my choices. How much of what I thought was *me* was actually mine? And how much of it had been shaped by societal norms and expectations?

This led me to an uncomfortable truth: I had built a life that looked successful on the outside, but it didn't truly align with the freedom I so deeply valued. I prided myself on being someone who wanted to spread his wings, to live without limits, but the reality was that I had created a golden cage for myself.

The big house, the nice things, the markers of success – all of it was part of a story I had been told. Someone, somewhere, had said, "This is what you need to do to be successful," and I believed them. I had followed the script without even realizing it, and in doing so, I had trapped myself in a life that didn't feel entirely my own.

This realization wasn't easy to face. It's not comfortable to admit that the life you've worked so hard to build doesn't fully align with who you are. However, that spark on the way to the cafeteria represented the beginning of my engagement with the different masks, a journey which, although difficult, has made my life immensely more profound.

What You Have Unmasked

I looked around and realized that I had been absorbing roles, rules, and realities that didn't belong to me. What are you now seeing as you look around? You've likely seen where systems have shaped your silence. Where religion wrapped itself around shame. Where "fitting in" meant erasing yourself. This chapter didn't just show you what's out there; it helped you reclaim what's within. You are not a product of society. You are a soul choosing how to show up in it.

CHAPTER 13

THE RAMIFICATIONS OF SOCIETAL MASKS

"Until you make the unconscious conscious,
it will direct your life and you will call it fate."
– Carl Jung

What You Will Unmask

Here, I'm confronting the masks society asked me to wear – the ones that came with labels, limitations, and lies about who I needed to be to belong. And as I lay them down, I'm inviting you to do the same. If you've ever felt like your truth made you too much or not enough ... this is where you begin to reclaim the truth of who you are, without apology. You'll start to see how societal roles can slowly chip away at our confidence, our creativity, and our connection, and how reclaiming your authenticity is not rebellion but remembrance. This is about breaking the contract you never signed and rewriting the one that aligns with who you've always been.

When we talk about societal masks, we're talking about layers of protection and adaptation that have built up over years, even decades, of living in a world that often demands conformity over authenticity. These masks aren't single entities but collections of personas and projections we've developed in response to external pressures, expectations, and the deep human need for acceptance and belonging.

The truth about these societal masks is that they weren't chosen; they were adopted as survival strategies, as ways to navigate a world that often feels unsafe for our authentic selves. From early childhood, we begin accumulating these layers: the "good child" mask to please our parents, the "cool kid" mask to fit in with our peers, the "professional" mask to succeed in school. Each layer adds to our protection and evolves as we age, but it also distances us further from our true nature.

These masks begin with good intentions. Perhaps you learned to suppress your natural enthusiasm because it was deemed "too much" by others, or you developed a persona of unwavering strength because showing vulnerability wasn't acceptable in your environment. These adaptations might have protected you once, serving as shields against judgment or rejection. But like a fortress built in peacetime, those walls now separate us from the very connections we seek.

The emotional toll of maintaining these societal masks is overwhelming, especially when you know you're wearing them. It's as if you're wearing a costume, one that's ill-fitting and heavy, every day of your life. It's draining, physically, mentally, emotionally, and spiritually, but we've convinced ourselves that it's necessary, that we need it to perform. In reality, we put so much effort into maintaining the performance and wearing our costume that we have little left for genuine connection or personal growth.

The exhaustion manifests in subtle ways at first, like a persistent sense of disconnection, a vague feeling of being an impostor in your own life, or a chronic low-grade anxiety about being "found out."

Yet, over time, these subtle manifestations can develop into more serious issues: depression that stems from disconnection from one's true self, anxiety disorders fueled by the constant pressure to maintain the mask, or a sense of emptiness and dysphoria that no external achievement seems to fill.

Perhaps nowhere is the impact of societal masks more evident than in our relationships. How can anyone truly know us if we're constantly presenting a curated version of ourselves?

These are a few examples of how this disconnection can manifest:

- The professional who maintains such a rigid boundary between their "work self" and "real self" struggles to form meaningful connections with colleagues.

- The parent who never shows vulnerability to their children unintentionally teaches them that emotions are something to be hidden.

- The partner who can't express their needs directly, instead hoping their significant other will somehow divine their true feelings through the careful performance they've constructed.

- And so many more …

The thing to remember is that when we put a mask on, we don't have to wear it forever. We don't have to be what other people expect us to be or do what they expect us to do. We can run and dance and sing and create and succeed in our own amazingly unique way, outside of societal expectations and pressures.

Our journey to authenticity starts with becoming aware of our masks and why we wear them.

MISMATCH

Like attracts like, but when we wear our masks, we tend to attract people who respond to *them* rather than our authentic selves, creating connections built on foundations of partial truths. We end up surrounded by people who love a version of us that isn't quite real, and that can be very isolating.

The masks we develop through our socialized societal experiences often come with the heaviest emotional toll because they're reinforced by entire communities and generations of tradition; they become both societal and cultural. Breaking free from them can feel like betraying not just expectations but our very heritage.

The weight of cultural masking is particularly heavy for those straddling multiple cultural identities, who must constantly switch between different masks to navigate various cultural contexts. This mismatch, the constant tension of maintaining a false self, can manifest itself physically.

Science shows us these possible physical manifestations:

- Chronic tension headaches from holding back true thoughts

- Digestive issues from swallowing words that need to be spoken

- Poor posture from trying to appear smaller or less noticeable

- Sleep disturbances from the mental effort of maintaining multiple personas

The overall physical impact goes beyond those obvious manifestations. The stress of maintaining inauthentic personas cancompromise our immune system, making us more susceptible to illness. The constant state of low-grade stress associated with masking can lead to elevated cortisol levels, which in turn can affect everything from our weight to our cardiovascular health.

Understanding these shadows doesn't mean we should dramatically cast off all our masks at once. These adaptations developed for reasons, often serving as necessary protection during vulnerable times in our lives. The goal isn't to discard these masks but to recognize them for what they are: temporary tools that may have outlived their usefulness.

The journey toward authenticity begins with gentle awareness. Notice the masks you wear in different situations. Observe how they feel in your body, how they affect your energy, and what they prevent you from expressing or experiencing. Start small. Allow one authentic reaction to show through in a safe situation. Share one true feeling with a trusted friend. The process of unmasking requires tremendous courage. It means facing the fears that led us to create these masks in the first place. It means risking rejection or disapproval. But it also offers the chance to live as our true selves, to connect authentically with others, and to contribute our unique gifts to the world.

Remember that these masks often began as acts of self-love or survival, even though they are potentially damaging when maintained too long. They're not evidence of weakness or falsehood but a testament to your ability to adapt and protect yourself. The key is recognizing when these protective measures have become prison walls and finding the courage to slowly, mindfully begin dismantling them.

The path is about recognizing that while these societal masks may have served us once, true fulfillment comes from unshackling ourselves from forced expectations, from choosing whether or not to bypass that yellow line.

A JOURNEY TO
AUTHENTIC SPIRITUALITY

As I traveled across five continents, visiting over 100 countries, I began to see something that fundamentally shifted my perspective: a pattern in how we envision and relate to the divine that reveals much about our societal conditioning.

What became clear to me is that the way we picture the divine isn't something that emerged naturally from within our cultures. It's a lens we inherited, often shaped by historical forces of power and control. In India, the divine looks Indian. In East Asia, Buddha bears Asian features. The gods and goddesses reflect the people who worship them. But when I traveled through Africa, I encountered a different reality that made me question everything about spiritual identity.

In African churches and homes, God didn't look African. The divine image was European – white skin, blue eyes, flowing hair. This wasn't merely about aesthetics; it spoke to something deeper about identity and self-worth. When you're taught from birth that the perfect being, the divine creator, looks nothing like you, it creates an underlying disconnect that shapes how you see yourself in relation to the sacred.

This is what masking docs at the most fundamental lcvcl. It subtly influences our sense of worth and belonging, extending across generations as we unconsciously pass these perceptions on to our children, expanding a cycle of spiritual disconnection.

In Africa, beneath the surface level of colonial religion, you find rich spiritual traditions where the divine wears African faces, where sacred power reflects the people themselves.Those traditions weren't erased; they were buried, forced underground, but preserved through resilience and determination.

What I want to make clear is that this process isn't about rejecting faith or tradition. Instead, it's about understanding how our spiritual self-image has been shaped by external forces and reclaiming our right to see ourselves in the divine.

When societies were colonized, their connection to their own divine image was often the first casualty. Controlling how people see God effectively controls how they see themselves.

Unmasking these religious layers requires us to question long-held beliefs and sit with uncomfortable truths. It means examining our most sacred assumptions and asking whether they truly serve our spiritual growth. The process might feel unsettling, but it opens the door to a more authentic relationship with spirituality.

When you realize that beneath the layers of religious conditioning lies the possibility of seeing the divine in your own image, that's when genuine transformation becomes possible.

The beauty in this unmasking process lies in how it leads not to rejection of spirituality but to a more authentic connection with it. My realizations allowed me to create a space for a genuine relationship with the divine to develop. I began to see that divinity and religion transcend any single image I or my society may have.

This kind of spiritual liberation isn't about finding the "right" image of God; it's about freeing ourselves from the limitations of any single representation. It's about reclaiming our ability to see ourselves in the divine and the divine in ourselves. Through this unmasking, we don't just change our religious perspective; we transform our fundamental understanding of our place in the spiritual landscape.

RECLAIMING IDENTITY AND CONFIDENCE

Few masks are as deeply ingrained as the Racial Mask. This mask is something society places upon us, subtly and persistently, until it becomes almost indistinguishable from our sense of self.

My moment of confronting this mask came in the most unexpected way: a missing iPad at a business mastery event in London.

It was the third day. We were working in groups and one of the attendees, a man who exuded success, complete with a shiny new iPad, realized it was gone. As the group began to look around, checking under chairs and asking if anyone had seen it, I froze. I was the only melanated person in the group, and I could feel a weight settle over me, pressing down with an unspoken but undeniable force. My mind raced, "They're going to think it was me."

No one said it out loud, but that was unnecessary. The silent question hung in the air: Did *he* take it?

At that moment, the Racial Mask I'd been conditioned to wear revealed itself fully. It was the mask of suspicion, of assumed guilt, of being seen as "less than." I knew the truth. I could've bought 100 iPads if I wanted to. But the mask didn't care about the truth. It whispered old, inherited fears: "Prove you're not what they think you are. Show them you're innocent." I even caught myself wanting to open my bag to prove I hadn't taken it, even though no one had accused me.

This is what the Racial Mask does. It doesn't just influence how others see us; it shapes how we see ourselves. It plants seeds of doubt, shame, and unworthiness, feeding off generations of societal narratives that label, stereotype, and diminish.

However, this unmasking meant turning inward, not outward. It wasn't about blaming the group or their glances, but about asking myself: *Why do I feel this way? Why am I carrying this weight?*

The work was hard. It took weeks of introspection to begin to peel back the layers of this mask. I had to go deep, confronting parts of myself that felt small, judged, and unworthy. I had to look at each of the narratives assigned to me because of my race and recognize how I had unconsciously accepted them.

Racial Masks show up in countless ways, shaping how we move through the world. They make us hesitate before speaking up, question whether we belong, or feel the need to prove ourselves over and over again. These masks are not of our making, but they have a way of becoming part of us if we don't confront them. They distort our identity, but the power of the mask wasn't in how others viewed me. It was in how much I let it influence how I viewed myself. And much like the way I reimagined my relationship with religion, in seeing my relationship with race for what it was, I was able to rewrite the narratives constraining me and forging my own identity,

Unmasking this deeply rooted layer of our identity is no small feat. It requires questioning the inherited beliefs and stories that have shaped us, confronting uncomfortable truths, and reclaiming the parts of ourselves we've hidden away. It's about understanding that the looks, the doubts, the suspicions – real or perceived – don't define us.

LEARNING ACROSS CULTURES

While traveling with my family, I began to notice the subtle ways Societal Masks shaped not just my perspective but also the experiences of my children. Of course, having raised my children in America, I was deeply aware of the persistent pervasiveness of racialization. However, visiting new places where we were often the only people who looked like us opened a new awareness. Societal conditioning wasn't just something we absorbed; it was something we unconsciously carried into the world, shaping how others saw us and how we saw them.

A turning point in how I approached these societal influences with my children was when we were traveling through Egypt, and our guide, Rag, invited us to have breakfast at his home before we continued on our journey. He explained that his wife needed a ride to the bus stop to visit her family, and he thought it would be a nice gesture to host us beforehand.

When we arrived, the home was humble but inviting. From the outside, it was simple. A brick structure with no paint, dirt paths leading to the front, and animals milling about nearby. Shoes were neatly lined up outside, as was their custom. The moment we stepped inside, everything shifted. The floors gleamed with a red tile finish, and the space was immaculate. We sat in a circle on the floor around a thick mat that served as their table, adorned with an array of freshly prepared dishes.

The hospitality was overwhelming in the best way. Chai tea, couscous, a variety of sauces – every dish was a reflection of their generosity. As we ate and exchanged stories through Rag's translations, there was a deep sense of connection forming. Yet, beneath this warmth, another layer of experience was unfolding.

Rag's wife wore a niqab, her entire face covered except for her eyes. For my daughters, especially my eldest, this was jarring. They were hesitant, their discomfort evident in the way they held themselves. It wasn't fear exactly – it was the weight of societal stereotypes they'd internalized, even at their young age.

Later, when we spoke about it, my daughter admitted that her reaction was tied to things she'd heard at school. Stories about bombings, terrorism, and danger associated with women who dressed like Rag's wife. I asked her, "Did you feel unsafe? Did anything about the experience make you think we were in danger?" She thought about it and shook her head. She admitted that her reaction wasn't rooted in reality; it was based on preconceived ideas she had never questioned before.

Later, something extraordinary happened.

Months later, we learned that Rag's wife had given birth to a baby girl. She named her Jasmine, after my daughter. This small act was a profound reminder of how connection can dismantle stereotypes. Just as my daughter had begun to unmask her societal conditioning, Rag's family was also unmasking theirs. They, too, had preconceived notions about Americans, particularly Black Americans. By simply being present and open, we challenged those perceptions and created a space for mutual understanding.

This experience proved that Societal Masks are universal, that everyone wears them in some form, shaped by culture, history, and the stories we're told. But it also proved the power of connection, of stepping into unfamiliar spaces with love and openness, to begin to peel back those layers.

Societal Masks often make us see only the differences in others. They magnify the 2% that separates us instead of focusing on the 98% of commonality we share as human beings. When we remove those masks, release those societal norms, and clear the biases that take root within us, we suddenly begin to create more authentic connections with one another. We strip away the performance, the stereotypes, the biases, the conditioning, and simply see the humanity.

When we approach others with love, curiosity, and an open heart, we create the space for transformation, not just within them but within ourselves. The Societal Masks we wear aren't permanent. They can be peeled back, one moment of connection at a time.

What You Have Unmasked

In this chapter, I shared the untangling of myself from society's expectations, and now you are untangling too. You've seen how some roles were assigned, not chosen ... how some definitions of "success," "strength," or "spirituality" were never yours to carry. You've started to remember that your identity isn't something to prove; it's something to embody. And in that remembering, you've reclaimed the courage to walk your truth in a world that often misunderstands it.

CHAPTER 14

UNMASKING THE ILLUSION THAT BURDENS SOCIETY

What You Will Unmask

In this chapter, I peel back the polished, practiced illusions we've been handed about what a "good life" looks like, and I invite you to look beneath the surface of what society celebrates. If you've ever felt disconnected even while "doing everything right," this chapter will speak directly to that ache. You'll begin to notice how systemic illusions about worth, identity, and belonging creep into your decisions without your permission. This is where we expose the invisible contracts we've unknowingly upheld ... and begin rewriting them from a place of alignment, truth, and radical self-trust.

Throughout this book, we've explored how Societal Masks shape our lives through personal stories and observations. But what does science tell us about these masks?

As it turns out, researchers have been studying this phenomenon for decades, though they might use different terms to describe it. Their findings not only validate what many of us have experienced but also help us understand why these masks are so powerful and persistent.

• The Power of the Group

One of the most striking discoveries about human behavior comes from Solomon Asch's experiments in the 1950s. To put yourself in the scenario laid out in this study, imagine being in a room with several other people, looking at two lines drawn on paper. One line is clearly longer than the other – there's no doubt about it – but everyone else in the room is saying the shorter line is longer. What would you do?

Asch found that many people would deny what their own eyes were telling them just to agree with the group. This isn't so different from how we adopt Societal Masks. We often suppress our true thoughts and feelings to align with what others expect of us, even when we know deep down that something doesn't feel right.

This tendency to conform gets even stronger when authority figures are involved. Stanley Milgram's famous studies showed that people would go to extraordinary lengths – even potentially harming others – when instructed to do so by someone they viewed as an authority. Think about how this plays out in our lives: how many of us have pursued careers, relationships, or lifestyles not because we wanted them, but because someone in authority, a parent, a teacher, society at large, told us we should?

• The Masks We Learn Early

Some of the most insightful research in this field comes from Kenneth and Mamie Clark's work with children in the 1940s. Their studies showed how children as young as three had already internalized society's biases, preferring white dolls over black ones regardless of their own race. This reflects what we discussed earlier about Racial Masks: how society's messages about worth and belonging start shaping us before we're even aware of it.

Claude Steele's research took this further, showing how these internalized beliefs actually affect our performance. When people are reminded of negative stereotypes about their group, they often perform worse on tasks – not because they're less capable, but because they're wearing a mask that tells them they can't succeed. Remember my story about the iPad at the business event? That was stereotype threat in action.

- **Different Cultures, Different Masks**

Richard Nisbett's research reveals something fascinating: the masks we wear aren't just about behavior; they actually influence how we see the world. He found that people from different cultures quite literally pay attention to different things when they look at the same scene. Western observers tend to focus on individual objects, while East Asian observers notice relationships and contexts more. This helps explain why our masks can feel so natural; they're not just covering who we are but shaping how we experience reality.

- **The Performance of Life**

Erving Goffman described social life as a kind of theater, where we're all performing different roles depending on our audience. This isn't necessarily negative. Sometimes, these performances help us navigate complex social situations. The problem comes when we forget we're performing and start believing the mask is our true face.

- **Religious Masks and Spiritual Identity**

Research undertaken by James Fowler helps us understand why Religious Masks can be particularly challenging to examine. Our spiritual beliefs often form during crucial periods of development, becoming deeply intertwined with our sense of self. This explains why questioning these beliefs can feel like questioning our very identity.

Social Science confirms what many of us have felt intuitively – these masks aren't just in our imagination. They're real psychological phenomena that affect how we think, feel, and behave. But understanding their reality also gives us hope. Just as these masks were learned, they can be unlearned. Just as they were created, they can be recreated or removed altogether.

Remember, the goal isn't to live completely without masks; even science suggests that some degree of social adaptation is healthy and necessary. The key is becoming conscious of our masks, understanding their origins and effects, and choosing mindfully which ones serve us and which ones we're ready to let go.

- **Nature's Lesson About Breaking Free**

Perhaps one of the most telling studies about societal conditioning comes from an unexpected place – research with rats by John B. Calhoun in his famous "Universe 25" experiments. Calhoun created what he called a "rat utopia" – a perfect environment with unlimited food, water, and space. Initially, the rats thrived. But as the population grew, they began developing strict social hierarchies and rigid behavioral patterns.

The most fascinating part? Even when the population declined and there was plenty of space and resources again, most rats continued their learned behaviors. They stuck to their established social rules and territories, even though these limitations were no longer necessary. However, a small group of rats, which Calhoun called "the beautiful ones," broke free from those patterns. They explored freely, created new behaviors, and lived differently from the rest.

Sound familiar?

Like these rats, we often maintain our Societal Masks long after they've served their purpose. We follow invisible lines on the floor even when no one's watching. But like Calhoun's "beautiful ones," we all have the capacity to break free from these conditioned patterns if we're willing to question them and chart our own course.

These are simply a handful of case studies that show the impact of and reason behind some of the masks we wear. But what they show is that while Societal Masks may be deeply ingrained, they're not permanent fixtures of who we are. They're learned responses that we can choose to unlearn, one conscious decision at a time.

What You Have Unmasked

I've let go of the belief that societal systems will ever fully see me. Have you? You've begun to spot the illusions for what they are: clever distractions that keep you performing instead of transforming. You've remembered that the truth isn't out there– it's inside. In your breath. In your knowing. Your sovereignty. And now, you've taken one step closer to living unmasked in a world still caught in performance.

Bibliography

Asch, S. E. (1951). Effects of group pressure upon the modification and distortion of judgments. *Journal of Abnormal and Social Psychology, 47(3), 382-389.*

Milgram, S. (1974). *Obedience to Authority: An experimental view.* Harper & Row.

Clark, K. B., & Clark, M. K. (1939). Racial identification and preference in children "The Doll Test".

Steele, C. M. (1997). A threat in the air: How stereotypes shape intellectual identity and performance. *American Psychologist, 52(6), 613-629.*

Nisbett, R. E. (2003). *The geography of thought: How Asians and Westerners think differently...and why.* Free Press.

Goffman, E. (1959). *The Presentation of Self in Everyday Life.* Doubleday.

Fowler, J. W. (1981). *Stages of Faith: The Psychology of Human Development and the Quest for Meaning.* Harper & Row.

Calhoun, J. B. (1973). The ecology and sociology of the Norway rat. In R. L. Calhoun (Ed.), *Behavioral Regulation of the Milieu.* Appleton-Century-Crofts.

Chapter 15

SOCIETAL UNMASKING AND HEALING

What You Will Unmask

We're moving into what it means to heal when the harm didn't start with us, when the pain was passed down, normalized, or disguised as culture, tradition, or success. This is where you begin to feel your way into truth without needing permission, apology, or proof. If you've ever felt torn between belonging and being yourself, this is where the tension breaks.
You'll learn how to hold grief and grace in the same hand ...
and how becoming whole doesn't mean fitting in;
it means finally standing out, on purpose.

Remember, your process for discovering your masks and removing them will be different from mine. This is a beautifully unique journey. However, these are some simple steps you can take to familiarize yourself with the Societal Masks that you might be wearing.

1. Recognize the Masks You Wear

The first step to unmasking societal influences, and other masks, is always awareness. Many of the roles and expectations to which we conform were never consciously chosen but were inherited from cultural norms, family expectations, or societal conditioning.

Those masks shape our identity, dictating how we present ourselves and what we suppress.

Ask yourself:

- What roles do you play in different areas of your life (work, relationships, social settings)?

- Which of these feel like an authentic expression of who you are, and which feel like obligations?

- Where in your life do you feel the most free? Where do you feel the most constrained?

Recognizing those masks allows you to begin questioning whether they serve you or limit you.

2. Identify the Origins of Your Conditioning

Once you've recognized the masks, it's important to trace them back to their roots. Understanding where they came from can help to loosen their grip.

Ask yourself:

- What beliefs about success, identity, or behavior were instilled in you growing up?

- Who or what influenced your understanding of what is "acceptable" or "successful"?

- When did you first start wearing this mask, and what purpose did it serve at the time?

Unpacking these origins allows you to see that many of these expectations were placed upon you rather than emerging from your own desires and values.

3. Notice When You Feel Inauthentic

Societal Masks create an internal disconnect. The more you suppress your true self to conform, the more exhausted and unfulfilled you may feel.

Reflect on:

- When do you catch yourself when you silence your true opinions or feelings out of fear of judgment?

- What parts of yourself do you hide or downplay because you worry they won't be accepted?

4. Reframe and Rewrite the Narrative

Many societal expectations have been unconsciously accepted as truth. But what if they aren't? What if success, identity, and belonging mean something different than what you've been taught?

Ask yourself:

- What if the way you've been measuring success isn't the only way?

- What would your life look like if you lived according to your own values rather than external expectations?

- How can you redefine these concepts in a way that feels true to you?

Rewriting the narrative allows you to reclaim control over how you define your life.

5. Express Your True Self in Small Ways

Unmasking doesn't have to be a drastic, overnight change. Small acts of authenticity can have a profound effect over time.

Consider:

- Speaking up when you would normally stay silent.

- Setting boundaries where you previously allowed societal expectations to dictate your choices.

- Exploring interests or passions you once suppressed.

Each step you take toward expressing your true self reinforces that you are not bound by societal constraints.

6. Surround Yourself with People Unconditioned by Societal Masks

Just as societal influences can shape us, so too can the people with whom we surround ourselves. Seek out those who encourage authenticity and celebrate individuality.

- Who in your life makes you feel seen and accepted?

- Are there relationships that feel transactional or based on maintaining a certain image?

- How can you create more space for real, unfiltered connection?

Authentic relationships reinforce that you are safe to be yourself without the need for performance.

7. Choosing the Masks That Work For You

Unmasking societal conditioning isn't about rejecting everything – it's about choosing with awareness. There may be aspects of societal norms that align with your values and others that you're ready to release.

Ask yourself:

- Which masks do you want to keep, and which do you want to shed?

- How can you align your daily actions with your true self?

- What steps can you take to ensure you're living by your own definition of fulfillment?

Living with intention means you are consciously choosing your path rather than following one that was handed to you.

Remember, unmasking is a process, not a destination!

There is no final moment when all masks disappear. Instead, it is an ongoing journey of self-discovery and self-expression. Each layer you remove brings you closer to living in alignment with who you truly are.

It's not always easy to look inward and reflect, especially when it has you questioning not only yourself but everything about the world around you. However, what is important to remember is that everyone and everything around you is also a product of their society, culture, and upbringing. They are all wearing their own masks, and as our world takes another step into the future, more and more people are becoming aware of the masks they wear and are also choosing to take them off.

It might feel daunting, uncertain, even scary, but trust me when I say that not only have you taken the first step by purchasing this book, but you are not alone in this journey. There are others just like you, some just starting their journeys, others partway through, but all show that when you do this, you can begin to live a truly incredible life.

RUMINATIONS ON
SOCIETAL INFLUENCE

We have already established that peeling back the Societal Masks we wear isn't easy. These masks have roots that dig deep into us, entwined with our thoughts, beliefs, and behaviours. They aren't just accessories we can casually discard; they've become part of our identity, and removing them feels like pulling away pieces of ourselves.

The process is delicate. You can try to rip the mask off all at once, but doing so is painful and can leave behind wounds that take longer to heal. A gentler, more intentional approach allows for awareness and care. And as you peel back each layer, you realize that this mask isn't something imposed by others; it's yours. You've worn it, maintained it, and, at times, allowed it to define you. The question then becomes: "Why am I taking it off?"

For me, this realization brought an unexpected shift. As I worked through my own layers, I began to respect those who chose to wear their Societal Masks with intention. These weren't people trapped by conditioning; they were individuals who understood their masks and wore them with grace and purpose. Their choice brought a sense of peace and order, a harmony in navigating the world while staying true to themselves.

Societal influences are all-encompassing. They shape us through race, gender, culture, sexual orientation, religion – any identity marker that the world uses to categorize and define us. These influences create tension between who we feel we are and who society tells us we should be. Across my travels and conversations with people from all walks of life,

I've seen this common struggle. No matter the "-ism" or societal structure at play, the internal battle is the same: This is **not** who I am and what I want to experience, but this is what my society expects of me and has **made** me.

Peeling away these influences doesn't happen in a single moment. Even as we remove the mask, there's often a residue left behind. Those lingering thoughts, behaviours, and expectations need to be cleared away. Healing the residue requires intentionality – it's not about rejecting masks entirely.

As I've discussed, masks can be tools, ways to navigate the world while staying true to our core. The difference lies in being proactive rather than reactive, intentional rather than conditioned. Living with sovereignty means choosing the masks you wear and understanding why you've chosen them.

Not everyone hears the call to unmask. For some, the bell remains silent. But for those who feel its pull, the journey is inevitable. It's a path of confronting the discomfort, questioning the norms, and stepping into a more expansive version of yourself.

Ultimately, healing Societal Masks is about reclaiming *your* place in this world. It's about choosing how you engage with society, how you express yourself, and how you navigate the complexities of life. The goal isn't to be mask-free but to live with intentionality, to wear only what serves your highest self. In doing so, you move from a reactive existence to one of sovereignty and alignment, embracing the fullness of your humanity.

What You Have Unmasked

You've touched the weight of wounds that weren't yours to carry and started to set them down. You've seen how systems shape suffering, but they can't touch your essence. Are you beginning to see yourself as a bridge between what was and what's possible? This part of the journey isn't about burning it all down; it's about rising from the ashes with clarity, compassion, and the courage to heal in public, so others know they can too.

PERSONAL LIBERATION BLUEPRINT – PART IV

There is a self that existed before the social script - before applause defined worth, before norms dictated expression, before institutions named what was "right." This is your original self. The part of you that remembers freedom as a birthright, not a reward.

But societal liberation doesn't mean rejecting community - it means reclaiming your place within it without distortion. This is where rebellion meets restoration. Where you stop performing and start participating as yourself. This blueprint is not detachment. It's realignment.

You are not just resisting. You are re-authoring.

Step 1: Identify the Masks You've Been Taught to Wear

What roles have you assumed to be accepted-professional, polite, productive, perfect?

Purpose: Creates awareness of social conditioning. Naming the mask is the first act of reclaiming your face.

Step 2: Notice Who Benefits from Your Performance

Who is served when you shrink, over-function, or self-abandon? What systems are upheld by your silence?

Purpose: Shifts your focus from personal shame to systemic influence. Liberation becomes a communal act.

Step 3: Recall a Time You Broke the Script

When did you speak out, opt out, or show up as your full self despite the risk? What happened to your body?

Purpose: Grounds courage in memory. Reminds you that authenticity is already within reach.

Step 4: Choose a Disruption Practice

What is one intentional act – saying no, dressing differently, naming truth – that helps you unlearn conformity this week?

Purpose: Embeds resistance into daily life. Turns awareness into embodied and meaningful defiance.

Step 5: Define What Freedom Feels Like for You

Forget theory – what does liberation feel like in your body, your choices, your day-to-day? Is it ease? Expression? Stillness? Power?

Write one sentence that begins: "For me, freedom feels like…"

Example: "…not second-guessing my truth, trusting my 'no,' and walking away without guilt."

Purpose: Personalises liberation. Reminds you that freedom is not one-size-fits-all-it's something you live, not just seek.

PART V
UNMASKING
THE COSMOS

LIVING UNIVERSALLY

"You are not IN the universe,
you ARE the universe,
an intrinsic part of it.
Ultimately, you are not a person,
but a focal point where the universe
is becoming conscious of itself."
Eckhart Tolle

CHAPTER 16

ENTERING THE COSMIC REALM

What You Will Unmask

This is where everything you thought was "out there" starts to feel deeply personal. The stars, the energy, the pull you've always felt toward something bigger – it's all been part of your design. You'll begin to sense that the cosmos isn't some distant force but a mirror. A memory. A map. If you've ever felt like you belonged to another world or that this one couldn't hold all of who you are, this is your invitation to stop shrinking and start expanding into your divine intelligence.
You're not crazy. You're cosmic.

Unmasking the cosmos is, without a doubt, the most enigmatic part of this book. It stretches beyond the tangible into the unseen. Writing this chapter felt like a leap of faith because cosmic consciousness, human design, universal energy … it's beautiful, of course, but it's also abstract.

I know how that can land for someone who's grounded in the survival of day-to-day life. Of bills, trauma, the hustle. How can you even begin to touch something like cosmic sovereignty when you're just trying to stay afloat?

To be honest, if you're struggling to meet your basic needs: food, shelter, stability, this may not feel relevant. You can't eat cosmic wisdom. I say that with respect because I've been there. And yet, I also know this truth: at some point on the journey, when you've moved through some of the earlier circles of unmasking, this layer begins to call you. Quietly, insistently. It's a deeper frequency.

The Cosmic Mask isn't about escape. It's about remembering. It represents the part of me that knows I am more than this body, this name, this story. It's the part of me that resonates with the rhythm of the stars, that feels guided by something bigger, even when I can't explain it. That part has always been there, even when I was in survival mode. I just couldn't always hear it over the noise.

This chapter, this circle, is not for rushing into. It will arrive when the body feels safe, when something within you is saying, "There's more." When it eventually does, you must remember: I am not separate. I am made of stardust and soil. I am human, yes, but I am also divine.

A JOURNEY INTO
THE MAGICAL COSMOS

As a child, I spent many holidays at my maternal grandmother's house, and my memories of that time are still as vivid as they were in the moment. It was a time filled with the warmth and wonder of childhood, but there was one moment that forever altered my understanding of life, spirit, and the unseen world.

I was about five years old, two years after my mom had passed away. I was still cocooned in my innocence, but I was curious enough, perhaps as a result of my mom's death, to sense there was more to existence than what meets the eye.

One night, I woke up shivering. The air in the room was icy, far colder than it should have been. There was an unusual stillness in the space, a strange hum in the silence, as if the very room was alive. That's when I noticed it. A swirl of smoke began seeping under the door. My breath hitched, and my body froze as I tried desperately to move. The smoke twisted and curled, forming a figure, feminine yet ethereal, gliding gently toward my bed.

The closer she got, the more clearly she seemed to form. Her face was faint, almost like a memory brought to life, and the wisps draped over her, flowing to the floor and filling the room with the chill of her presence. But it was her feet that caught my attention. The smoke had shaped itself into shoes – one of them with a loose buckle, dangling as if forgotten in haste.

My heart raced, and my palms were slick with sweat despite the cold. But as she sat on the edge of my bed and reached out, a wave of calm washed over me. Her touch, if that's what it could be called, felt light, like a soft breeze against my skin.

166

"Don't be afraid. You are safe."

I didn't question it. I didn't need to. A deep sense of knowing settled over me, as if this presence had always been there, watching over me, waiting for the moment I might need her. Minutes, or perhaps only seconds, passed before she moved away, her form flowing back toward the door. The smoke trailed behind her, disappearing under the crack as silently as it had arrived.

I laid there, stunned but inexplicably at peace. The calm she left with me lingered, and I soon drifted back to sleep.

The next morning, I couldn't keep the experience to myself. I ran to my grandmother, spilling every detail – the icy air, the swirling smoke, the loose buckle on the shoe. She listened intently, her eyes soft.

When I finished, she simply said, "That was your mother."

Her words left me breathless.

"How?"

"She comes sometimes," my grandmother said gently. "Especially when you're here with me. She just wants to make sure you're okay." She smiled, a light laugh escaping her lips, "You know she used to wear her shoes like that, never buckled the straps. It was her little thing."

That one detail, so uniquely her, made it undeniable. The presence I'd felt: the figure who had calmed me, truly was my mother. Even though I couldn't grasp the how or why, I wasn't afraid. Instead, I felt comforted, seen, and protected.

That was my first glimpse into the unseen, into a world that exists beyond what our eyes can perceive.

LOST IN THE JAMAICAN STARS

My first experience with the cosmos wasn't something I sought out – it was an awakening. After that night, I was drawn to the stars like they were calling me. The darkness in Jamaica was thick, pressing down on the land like a vast, endless blanket. With no city lights or distractions, the night sky became my own kind of entertainment, my Netflix.

I'd lie on the cool grass, staring up at the stars, letting time slip away. I felt like I was moving with them, leaping from one to the next, moving through space and time like a river between the rocks. In those moments, I wasn't bound to the earth. My body was there, but *I* was somewhere else. I called it "Star Hopping."

Whenever I did it, there was a dizzying sensation, like the universe was pulling me into something truly limitless. Somehow, the answers to questions I had about life, about myself, about everything were just *there,* not spoken, not explained, but *felt*. The stars, with their quiet rhythm, carried a wisdom beyond anything I'd learned or could learn confined to the earth.

It wasn't just the sky that captivated me; it was the feeling that everything around me was part of something bigger. The grass beneath my hands, the wind through the trees, the distant hum of crickets – everything was connected. Even the smallest ant beside me had a place in this grand design. I didn't have the language for it then, but I *knew*. The universe wasn't something far away; it was intertwined with me, with all of life.

As I lay there, staring up at the stars, my mind would wander, asking all sorts of questions that seemed bigger than anything I could comprehend. "Why are we here? Why is there so much anger and pain? Is there anything I need to do about it? What role do I play in this game of life?"

At five years old, those mindless ponderings that draw us toward a deeper understanding were questions I didn't fully know I was asking. But something that I would ask, something that I knew I wanted to know the answer to, even back then, was, "What is my mom doing now?"

The stars felt like they were listening. I didn't need to hear their response, but in those moments, I could almost feel the universe speaking to me in ways words couldn't capture. It wasn't an answer I would find in books or from anyone else; it was something I had to discover for myself. And with each passing night, under that endless sky, I felt closer to uncovering whatever truths lay hidden in the vastness of the cosmos. I even felt closer to my dear mother.

As I closed my eyes, the stillness wrapped around me. I wasn't trying to understand it, and I didn't have to; I was just *in* it. In sync. And in that presence, I found something deeper than thought, deeper than logic – I found peace. I wasn't just observing the universe; I was part of it.

I didn't know it at the time; how could I? But that was when I first realized that the cosmos isn't something outside of us; it *is* us. The same rhythms that move the stars move within me. And in that vastness, I wasn't lost; I was home.

REDISCOVERING THE COSMOS

As a child, the cosmos wasn't an abstract concept or a faraway expanse; it was a part of me. It was a time when the universe felt so close, so alive, that it seemed to breathe with me. I moved through life immersed in that vast oneness, feeling the rhythm of something infinite. It wasn't something I thought about; it was something I knew; it's something all of us know, whether we realize it or not.

As we grow older, that connection begins to fade. Life, with all its demands and expectations, creeps in and slowly severs that connection. The world lays out a path, and we follow it without question. There are roles to fulfill, boxes to check, rules to obey … The sense of wonder and unity that once came so naturally begins to feel like a distant memory. Piece by piece, we drift away from that cosmic dance that was once our constant companion.

It isn't an abrupt loss but a gradual drift, like a boat carried by a slow, unrelenting current. The things we begin to align ourselves with, the beliefs, the rituals, the structures, aren't rooted in our experience. They aren't a reflection of our true selves. They are handed to us, pre-approved and wrapped in expectations.

For me, faith became something I followed because I was told to, not something I felt. I did what was required: I went to church, played the roles of a "good" person, a diligent student, and an aspiring entrepreneur. But the more I conformed to what I thought I should be, the further I strayed from who I actually was.

That shift, the loss, was not something I noticed at first. Like many others, I was simply too busy chasing what the world told me mattered: achievements, recognition, success. By nine years old, I was already chasing the next project, the next idea, the next goal.

As the years passed, I built a life that looked impressive from the outside – a growing business, a family, a carefully curated version of success. But no matter how much I achieved, there was always a quiet ache inside me, an emptiness that no amount of accomplishments could fill.

It was a moment I hadn't anticipated – a simple prompt during an explorative seminar. The facilitator asked us to go back, way back, to our earliest memory. I didn't know where my mind would take me, but I let myself surrender to the process. And then, like a wave crashing against the shore, it all came rushing back.

I was under those stars again, lying in the cool grass as a child, staring into infinity. The memory wasn't distant or hazy; it was vivid, alive, and all-encompassing. I could feel the earth beneath me, the night air brushing against my skin, the vastness of the sky wrapping around me like a familiar embrace.

It wasn't just a memory. It was a homecoming.

Then, as if a dam had broken, more memories began to flood in. Moments with my mom before she passed, tiny details I hadn't thought about in years. Even fragments I didn't know I had came to life, each carrying an emotional weight that left me breathless. At 32, these recollections hit harder than I could've imagined, each one layered with meaning I was only beginning to understand.

There was a strange urgency tied to these memories, one I hadn't fully acknowledged until that moment. I realized that because my mom had died at 33, somewhere deep in my subconscious, I had adopted the belief that my life was on the same timer. Without realizing it, I had been living as though I had to accomplish everything before that age, as though my time was running out.

It felt like a cosmic alignment, almost too perfect to ignore. My wife was pregnant with our third child, just months away from giving birth, and here I was, standing at a crossroads of memory, emotion, and impending change. The past, present, and future seemed to converge in that moment, and for the first time, it all started to make sense.

Those memories weren't random; they were messages. They had been stored, safeguarded within me, and now they were surfacing, as if the universe knew I was ready to receive them. And it wasn't just my memories. Some felt ancient, as though they belonged to my ancestors, carried forward through blood and spirit. Others seemed larger than life, cosmic in their nature, as if they were etched into the fabric of the universe itself.

SYNTHESIZING MY SOUL WITH THE COSMOS

Through meditation, I began tapping into something beyond myself. Waiting just beyond everything I knew were guides, ancestors, and cosmic energies; each one waiting patiently for me to remember. It was as if they had always been there, holding space until the day came when we would reconnect. As my awareness expanded, I found myself asking, "How could I have forgotten this?"

The cosmos isn't just a collection of distant stars and planets. It's a force that connects and shapes everything. The moon pulls the tides, just as it influences the water within us, aligning our rhythms with its own. Ancient cultures understood that. With no regard for the geographical location, they lived by these cycles, recognizing the deep relationship between the heavens and the earth. We are not separate from the cosmos; we *are* the cosmos, made of the same elements, moving to the same unseen currents.

That moment of rediscovery ignited a hunger to better understand not only myself but the universe and the countless unseen patterns that shape our lives. I dove into hidden knowledge, exploring anything that might offer clarity.

Neuro-linguistic programming (NLP) helped me unlearn patterns that no longer served me. Carl Jung's work on archetypes and the collective unconscious gave language to the patterns I had sensed for years. Jung's concept of the *Animus* and *Anima* resonated deeply, illuminating the interplay of masculine and feminine energies within me. However, this journey wasn't just intellectual; the body had to be engaged as well. Breathwork, meditation, ecstatic dance, tapping, and somatic practices unlocked connections I hadn't known were there.

173

The Hermetic principle, "as above, so below; as within, so without," transformed from an abstract idea into something I could *feel*. Everything began falling into place; it was like playing a game of Tetris, and the journey took me to places I had only imagined, immersing me in wisdom that reshaped my understanding of existence. Weeks in the Amazon, spiritual practices in Brazil, and the ancient traditions of Gabon weren't just experiences; they were initiations and invitations to remembrance. Remembering that the cosmos isn't distant. It's alive in the ancient stones, the flowing rivers, and the pulse of our own hearts.

Recently, my wife asked, "If you weren't doing what you do now, what would you want to be?"

Without hesitation, I answered, "An archaeologist."

I've always been drawn to the ancient, whether in the physical, metaphysical, or spiritual. There's something about touching history, feeling the energy of what came before, that feels like touching the cosmos itself. Archaeology isn't just the practice of uncovering and recording the past; it's not about digging up ancient history and isolating it to its time period. It is the practice of grounding the wisdom of the present in the past so that the future can learn from it.

At its core, this unmasking journey is about one thing: *remembering*. Remembering that we are not separate from the universe but an integral part of its vast, intricate design. Each insight, each practice, each memory has been a step toward uncovering who I truly am.

The cosmos is not a puzzle to be solved; it's a relationship to be nurtured. Within each of us lies the infinite, a truth as old as the stars and as immediate as the breath we take. We are not trying to chase answers or reach the tallest peak by taking this journey; we are learning to live with our questions, allowing them to guide us back to ourselves.

What You Have Unmasked

*You've begun to remember what your soul has always known:
you are woven into the rhythm of the universe. The longing
you've felt wasn't emptiness; it was the call to reconnect.
You've stepped beyond logic and into knowing, beyond the five
senses and into the frequency of remembrance.
The cosmos isn't above you; it's within you.
And your journey home has already begun.*

Bibliography

Jung, C. G. (1981). *The Archetypes and the Collective Unconscious* (2nd ed.). Princeton University Press.

Three Initiates, (1908) *The Kybalion: A Study of the Hermetic Philosophy of Ancient Egypt and Greece.* Yogi Publication Society.

CHAPTER 17

THE CUMULATIVE BURDEN OF OUR COSMIC MASKS

What You Will Unmask

*You've unmasked the child, the lineage, the society. Now it's
time to unmask the cosmos – not the stars, but the stories
you've written across them. This is where the deeper layers
surface, the ones so ancient they feel like they didn't even start
with you. If you've ever felt a burden you couldn't name or a
weight that didn't match your life's timeline, this is where it
starts to make sense. You'll uncover the cosmic imprints, soul
contracts, and patterns you've carried unknowingly.
This isn't about blame; it's about liberation.*

Your birth isn't random; it's a precise intersection of universal
energies, and when you enter this world, you carry energy imprints
as unique as your fingerprints. These cosmic signatures are formed
by the precise moment and environment of your birth and guide
your life's journey. They're not predetermined destiny, but they
create the road map – every possibility, opportunity, and potential
that awaits you.

These signatures are like silent conductors, orchestrating your actions, reactions, and relationships. They are at the forefront of our lives but often go unnoticed, overshadowed by the noise of our experience. But, while they are not like physical fingerprints you can see or touch, you can consciously choose to become aware of these energy frequencies.

Unmasking Cosmic healing is more than a healing process; it's an invitation to tap into those energies and to those beyond to the infinite energy that connects everything. It is the process of finding balance, reconnecting with a divine spark that already resides within each of us.

When we ignore this cosmic connection, life can feel empty and directionless. We become trapped in cycles of lack – financial, material, emotional, spiritual. But the abundance we seek, the solutions to our deepest struggles, are already stored within this cosmic energy, waiting to be awakened.

Unmasking the cosmic is to align with your infinite potential. It's about rediscovering the oneness we share with creation and living vibrantly, intentionally, and deeply connected. This isn't just a spiritual concept; *it's your birthright*. To heal cosmically is to awaken, to thrive, and to reclaim the fullness of life that has always been waiting for you.

WALKING THROUGH THE UNIVERSE

Something that I need to address is the dual impact of wearing the Cosmic Mask. Shedding it can bring a deeper awareness and a strengthened connection with the divine infinite, it can also create the illusion of separation. In its vast expanse, it fosters the idea of independence as though you exist apart from the intricate web of life – the belief that you are an isolated individual, disconnected from others and the universe. But this perspective limits your understanding of yourself and your role in the world.

Unmasking allows you to shift and realize you are not a detached and directionless particle, part of a thread in the fabric of existence, connected to everyone and everything. This awareness changes your outlook entirely. You focus on helping rather than harming, giving rather than taking, and loving rather than hating. Love becomes the wave that carries you, expansive and binding, while anger is the fragmented state of the particle: reactive and isolated.

The Cosmic Mask also affects how you view the world. When it's on, it narrows your perspective, making you feel isolated in your struggles and unaware of the broader connection you share with others. It's the belief that no one has known hardship as you have, that no one understands what you are going through, and can lead to fear-driven behaviours rooted in self-preservation and scarcity.

When you're wearing the Cosmic Mask, it's easy to believe that "no one is coming to save you," that you're entirely on your own and must carry every burden yourself. But while there's truth in taking responsibility for your own growth, this belief blinds you to the vast support and connection available to you.

As you begin to unmask, a deeper understanding unfolds. You realize that while no one may "save" you in the traditional sense, you are never truly alone. Energies, frequencies, and unseen partnerships are always present, ready to guide and assist you. Removing the mask is like clearing the static, allowing you to recognise the vast network of support you didn't see before.

In unmasking, your worldview expands. You understand that your choices ripple outward into the collective, and you approach life with trust, collaboration, and abundance. You begin to see the divine spark in everyone and approach others with empathy and compassion, recognising their journey as part of the same interconnected whole. It shifts you from resistance to flow, aligning you with the natural rhythm of life.

The Cosmic Mask represents disconnection – separation from your higher self, from the guidance of spirit, and from the larger flow of life. Shedding it creates space for reconnection with your natural, authentic self, with those around you, with the unseen guides, and with your purpose. It opens the doorway to partnerships, insight, and alignment that were always there, waiting to be accessed.

Removing the Cosmic Mask helps you balance individuality with connectedness. It reminds you that your life has value simply because you are part of the greater whole. Through this process, you rediscover your authentic self and also your place in the cosmos and the shared truths that unite us all.

EXPLORING THE ALTERNATIVES

Choosing not to take off the Cosmic Mask, like any mask, can feel like an easier path. By keeping our masks on, we live a life of blissful ignorance, like a satisfied pig, so to speak. There's certainly a comfort in keeping your head down, but even in that state, pain is inevitable. The difference isn't in whether we experience pain but in how we move through it. With the mask off, we can navigate with greater awareness rather than letting the mask define us.

In my own journey, I approached cosmic healing with intention and openness. Wherever I traveled, I made it a practice to sit with elders, absorbing their wisdom, not as an outsider looking in, but as a student in the presence of those who had spent lifetimes tending to knowledge far older than any book. Often, they knew why I was there before I even spoke and guided me toward insights I wouldn't have reached on my own.

I had an extraordinary encounter with the Bwiti people in Gabon, West Africa. I spent time in their company, immersing myself in their ancient initiation practices. With their elders' guidance, I was introduced to Iboga, a sacred plant medicine that opens doorways to cosmic understanding. The experience revealed layers of my existence I had never touched before. It felt as if I were accessing the Akashic Records themselves, tapping into that ancient reservoir of universal memory and truth. My time in Ghana and South America only deepened that understanding. It was there that I truly grasped the interplay of light and dark, the cosmic rhythm that shapes all things.

But that kind of access demands balance. It's like stepping into a banquet where every dish ever conceived is laid before you. If you try to consume it all at once, you'll overwhelm yourself. The lesson was patience, taking in only what was necessary, allowing the rest to unfold in its own time.

Yet, while experiences like these can act as a back door into cosmic awareness, they are not the only way. There is also a front door, a slower, more intentional path that demands discipline, consistency, and presence. While I might have entered through the back door, it was by the front door that I was able to ground everything and strengthen my initial revelations. It assured me that the understanding I gained was not borrowed but built, not dependent on external catalysts but forged through effort and endurance.

Everyone's journey unfolds in its own way. For example, in many traditional settings, no external tools are used at all, only the energy of the space, the intention of the seeker, and the wisdom of those who have come before. I've observed that those who rely too heavily on shortcuts often struggle to access the same depths without them. The key lies in integration – taking what resonates, releasing what does not, and building a foundation that remains solid long after the initial awakening.

For me, this process is ongoing. I've learned to hold lessons lightly, keeping them within reach rather than clinging to them rigidly. Some insights take years to ripen, returning only when you are ready to understand them in a new way. Cosmic healing should not be seen as a race … it is a beautiful, rewarding journey.

TO THE SCEPTIC

To the cosmic sceptical, I hear you. For a long time, I struggled to attach myself to these ideas. But there is something there, and if you're curious about unlocking it, here's where you can begin.

The first step is acknowledging that all is mental. You have to open your mind to the possibility that something larger than yourself exists. Think of it like trying to explain the colour red to someone who's never seen it – it's nearly impossible unless they're willing to *experience* it for themselves. That experience involves having a belief in the infinite and in the perceived impossible. But your red will never be the same as my red, and so this journey requires an openness to the unknown, a willingness to say, "There's more out there than I've allowed myself to see."

If you close yourself off, judging or dismissing these ideas outright, you block the resonance that allows you to align with greater awareness. However, if you embrace the possibility, even tentatively, you will start to shift. This shift is when the unlocking begins.

There's a saying: "When the student is ready, the teacher will appear." That teacher doesn't always show up as a person. Sometimes, it's synchronicities – a series of seemingly coincidental events that provide exactly what you need. It might be as simple as stumbling across a YouTube video with a message that feels like it was meant just for you or seeing a rainbow shine through the clouds after you've been walking through the rain for the longest time. It's that feeling of hope that there is not only something better but also something more, that when you take that next step, there is something else waiting for you.

That is how it starts, and once it starts, it doesn't stop.

What You Have Unmasked

You've started to see the difference between what belongs to you and what was borrowed, absorbed, or inherited through lifetimes. You've recognized that some masks weren't built in this body or this lifetime, but your soul still said yes to healing them. And now, you've chosen to stop the cycle, not just for yourself but for every version of you that ever existed. You're no longer held hostage by the cosmic weight; you're learning to dance with it.

CHAPTER 18
UNRAVELING
THE HUMAN DESIGN

What You Will Unmask

Here, we go inward to go upward. Human Design isn't just a system; it's a sacred reminder that you were created with precision, purpose, and poetry. You'll begin to see how your patterns weren't random, how your wiring was never broken – it was encoded. If you've ever struggled to understand yourself, felt out of sync with the world, or doubted your instincts, this will feel like coming home. You're not flawed. You're formatted. And your soul has always known the code.

Through the process of cosmic unmasking, we heal. As we heal individually, we tap into the universal rhythms that guide and sustain life. This isn't a journey of discovery but of rediscovery, as everything we uncover is already a part of who we are. It is our essence, free from the distortions of conditioning and expectation.

As I mentioned earlier, one powerful tool for this unmasking is **Human Design**, a system that reveals how our energy is naturally meant to flow, offering a road map back to our most authentic selves. It integrates elements of astrology, the I Ching, Kabbalah, the chakra system, and quantum physics, and it offers a practical framework for self-awareness.

Many people focus on what steps they need to take without questioning why they pursue certain goals. Human Design encourages reflection, allowing you to step back and realign with your authentic nature instead of forcing you into predefined roles. Some traditions, such as African spiritual systems, pass down wisdom in structured, almost step-by-step ways. Human Design recognizes that these journeys unfold differently for each person, which is why self-awareness, the mantra "Know thyself," is at the core of this system.

At the heart of Human Design are **nine energy centers** that influence how we process information, emotions, and experiences. These centers function like an internal operating system, shaping the way we interact with the world. Some are defined, meaning they operate in a consistent and reliable way, while others remain open, allowing for fluidity and adaptation based on external influences.

For example, **The Head Center, Crown Center, and Ajna Center** form the upper triangle, governing inspiration, pressure, and conceptual thinking. When these are defined, an individual has a fixed way of processing ideas. If they are open, there is an ability to absorb and explore different perspectives. Society often expects everyone to be a consistent thinker, which can create unnecessary pressure for those who are naturally designed to be fluid in their thought processes.

The Heart Center (Ego) is much more defined. It regulates willpower and self-worth. Those with an undefined Heart Center are not meant to be consistently willful or prove their worth through external validation. However, societal conditioning often instills the belief that effort and achievement must be constant, leading to burnout and feelings of inadequacy.

Through its process, Human Design categorizes individuals into **four types**, each with a unique way of engaging with the world. Understanding and embracing this natural strategy allows for greater ease and alignment in life.

- **Manifestors** (9% of the population) are designed to initiate and act independently. Many suppress their leadership instincts due to societal conditioning that encourages seeking permission. Embracing their power requires learning to inform others of their actions rather than waiting for approval.

- **Generators & Manifesting Generators** (70%) thrive by responding to life rather than forcing outcomes. Their sacral energy is designed to engage with what excites them. Many Generators, however, push themselves into initiation, disregarding their natural flow and creating unnecessary frustration. Trusting life's invitations leads to greater fulfillment.

- **Projectors** (20%) are designed to guide and direct energy, but their effectiveness relies on being recognized and invited. Many Projectors overextend themselves in an attempt to keep up with energy types that are more suited for constant activity. Embracing their need for rest and selective engagement allows them to operate at their highest potential.

- **Reflectors** (1%) are mirrors of their environment, reflecting the health of their surroundings. With no defined centers, they are designed to adapt and shift based on the energy around them. Societal pressure to be consistent often conflicts with their natural design, which thrives on change and fluidity.

Alongside these "types," Human Design provides **an authority** – a built-in decision-making strategy that helps individuals make choices in alignment with their true nature. Many of the heaviest masks we wear stem from societal expectations around decision-making.

- **Emotional Authority** requires patience, as clarity comes through experiencing emotional waves over time. Society often encourages quick decisions, leading many to override their natural process. Honoring emotional clarity results in better-aligned choices.

- **Sacral Authority** operates through gut instincts. Those with this authority are meant to trust their immediate bodily response, yet many fall into overanalyzing situations instead of following their natural energy cues.

- **Splenic Authority** functions through instant knowing, a quiet whisper of intuition that does not repeat itself. Societal norms favor logical explanations, making it difficult for those with Splenic Authority to trust decisions that come without tangible reasoning

But unmasking through Human Design is not about changing who you are; it is about returning to your natural state, becoming aware of where conditioning and misalignment have impacted you, and allowing you to make that conscious shift back into authenticity.

So, as you start to unmask, to connect with *your* unique design:

- **Start with your type:** Are you honoring your natural strategy, or are you forcing yourself into a role that does not align with your design?

- **Observe your authority:** Are your decisions guided by your innate decision-making process, or are external influences dictating your choices?

- **Notice your defined and undefined centers:** Where have you been trying to be consistent when you are designed to be fluid? Where have you been suppressing aspects of yourself that are naturally fixed?

This can provide you with a precise and personal map for self-awareness. It highlights where conditioning has created masks and offers a framework for returning to an authentic way of being.

THE 9 CENTERS

- **Head Center (Crown)** – Inspiration, pressure to think, mental questions

- **Ajna Center** – Conceptualization, mental processing, and certainty

- **Throat Center** – Communication, manifestation, self-expression

- **G Center (Identity)** – Direction, love, identity, sense of self

- **Heart Center (Ego)** – Willpower, value systems, material matters

- **Spleen Center** – Intuition, survival instincts, health awareness

- **Sacral Center** – Life force energy, sexuality, work capacity

- **Solar Plexus Center** – Emotions, desires, feelings

- **Root Center** – Pressure, stress, adrenaline, physical drive

What You Have Unmasked

You've started to decode the blueprint that's been living inside you all along. What once felt like struggle now looks like structure. What felt like chaos now reveals a deeper choreography. You've stopped trying to be who you're not and started to trust how you were made.
This isn't about becoming something new.
It's about finally aligning
with what's been divinely designed.

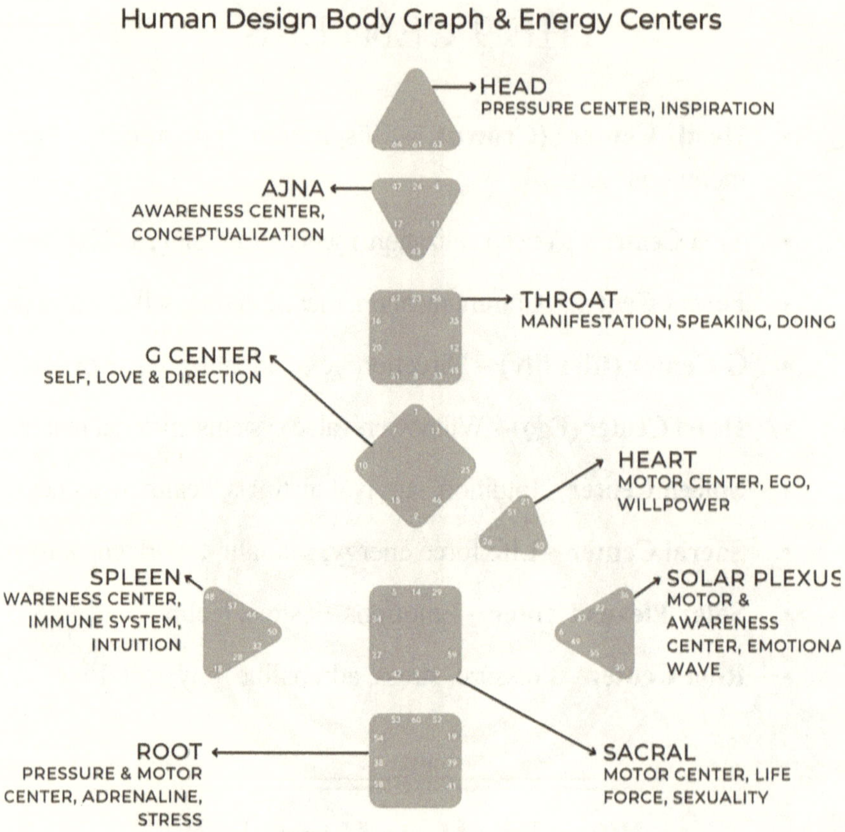

Human Design Body Graph & Energy Centers

HEAD
PRESSURE CENTER, INSPIRATION

AJNA
AWARENESS CENTER,
CONCEPTUALIZATION

THROAT
MANIFESTATION, SPEAKING, DOING

G CENTER
SELF, LOVE & DIRECTION

HEART
MOTOR CENTER, EGO,
WILLPOWER

SPLEEN
WARENESS CENTER,
IMMUNE SYSTEM,
INTUITION

SOLAR PLEXUS
MOTOR &
AWARENESS
CENTER, EMOTIONA
WAVE

ROOT
PRESSURE & MOTOR
CENTER, ADRENALINE,
STRESS

SACRAL
MOTOR CENTER, LIFE
FORCE, SEXUALITY

"Human Design Body Graph & Energy Centers" diagram

You can analyze
your own human
design here…

CHAPTER 19
UNMASKING COSMIC HEALING

What You Will Unmask

You've done the inner work. You've traveled the ancestral
road. You've lifted the societal veil. And now, you learn to heal
not just from memory, but from the Mystery. This is where
healing becomes multidimensional and where energy moves
before words. When you stop asking "How do I fix this?" and
begin asking "What wants to be transmuted through me?"
You'll step into the sacred truth that your presence is medicine.
That healing doesn't have to look hard, loud,
or dramatic to be real. Sometimes, it's subtle.
Sometimes, it's cosmic.
And sometimes, it's already done.

Unmasking Cosmic Healing restores balance and alignment across
every dimension of our being: physical, emotional, mental, and
spiritual. Rooted in ancient wisdom, this unmasking reawakens our
connection to the universe beyond mere self-help rhetoric and reunites
us with the purest form of ourselves.

By tuning into cosmic flows, we shed false identities that tether us to misalignment. These masks, constructed from societal expectations and personal fears, prevent us from experiencing the fullness of our authentic selves. When we let go, we undergo a kind of metamorphosis that allows us to step fully into harmony with the broader existential landscape.

The cosmos represents the sum total of our existence. It provides the ultimate zoom-out moment, revealing a perspective that transcends the immediacy of our current experience. More than a physical space, the cosmos embodies the energy, essence, and existence that preceded our birth and continues beyond our comprehension.

Even before our physical conception, elements of our being were already in play. It's a deeper reality that penetrates the energy frequencies of existence itself, and our understanding of it can never truly comprehend its infinity. However, we can begin to tap into that understanding, and with consciousness awareness, we can grow that understanding to deepen our cosmic connection.

This cosmic connection demands a radical shift in perspective, one that almost requires us to abandon the notion of individuality. As I've discussed, our Cosmic Mask creates an illusion of separation, but as we unmask it, we recognize ourselves as an integral part of the larger whole. Remember, we are not isolated particles but a single part of a thread connected to a much larger weave.

NAVIGATING THE UNSEEN

Societal expectations have almost ingrained the concept of control into every one of us. We *need* to have control in our lives in order to feel safe and secure. Whether we earn enough to be financially secure or have enough people to be socially secure, our lives are centered around the idea of control.

However, engaging with cosmic energies isn't about control but about alignment. It demands careful discernment and intentionality, or else we risk walking aimlessly in its infinite expanse. This engagement is not a process we can control or manipulate; we cannot influence the cosmic flow. That would be like trying to change the flow of a river when you're already in its stream.

Ancient cultures understood this complexity, often preserving cosmic teachings through oral traditions rather than written texts. Experiences of the cosmos are inherently personal, with identical energies potentially evoking entirely different insights depending on the individual.

This journey is not a universal prescription with a single path, solution, or answer; it is an intimate process of discovery and resonance that defies simple explanation. It is an experience to be felt rather than described. Words become insufficient, barely touching the essence of the experience. Yet, for those willing to open themselves, the journey reveals truths that transcend physical perception, connecting us to the fundamental source of creation.

POWER OF THE GROUP

While unmasking is often personal, cosmic unmasking is most powerful when experienced through shared rituals. Collective experiences heighten transformation by fostering deep connection and self-awareness. These can include ancient practices like Shipibo ayahuasca ceremonies in Peru or Bwiti iboga rituals in Gabon, both of which use sacred plant medicines in guided settings to facilitate profound introspection.

In Shipibo tradition, ayahuasca ceremonies are led by a curandero (healer) who sings "icaros" – sacred songs – while participants drink a visionary plant brew. The experience helps to shed illusions and access deeper awareness. Bwiti iboga rituals, meanwhile, use the psychoactive iboga root in ceremonies marked by drumming, chanting, and storytelling, guiding individuals through intense self-exploration and ancestral connection.

These are not abstract spiritual "woo woo" concepts but tangible, time-honored practices actively curated to dissolve barriers and reveal deeper truths about the self and the universe.

While a solo meditation retreat might reveal personal insights, the dynamics of group ceremonies create unique conditions for transformation. Picture twenty people seated in a ceremonial maloka (an ancestral long house built by indigenous people of the Amazon). The combined energies and forces support individuals to bypass their rigid analytical mind and experience normally hidden psychological thoughts and subjects.

For those seeking alternatives to traditional plant medicines, other specific practices offer powerful doorways: holotropic breathwork's intensified breathing patterns, authentic movement's spontaneous physical expression, or even the joys of unbounded somatic dancing.

Each modality provides concrete tools for exploring consciousness.

The effectiveness lies in the precision of these time-tested methods. When a Shipibo maestro whistles an icaro or a Bwiti initiate plays the mungongo mouth bow, they're working with specific frequencies and patterns that facilitate particular states of consciousness. These aren't vague "energy practices" but sophisticated technologies developed through centuries of careful observation.

In such environments, participants often report precise phenomena: geometric visual patterns, encounters with archetypal figures, or somatic releases accompanied by spontaneous movements. The cosmic becomes tangible through direct experience rather than theoretical understanding.

This work grounds abstract concepts in lived experience. Instead of solely discussing unity, participants can directly see the electromagnetic fields connecting all life. Instead of philosophizing about ego death, they may experience temporary dissolution of self-boundaries while remaining within the safety of a group.

Group practices and ceremonies are truly invaluable. They offer us precise tools for navigating non-ordinary states, turning philosophical ideas into real-life realities.

COSMIC ALCHEMY
AND UNIVERSAL COVENANTS

The journey of spiritual transformation, or cosmic alchemy, goes beyond the traditional metaphor of magically transforming lead into gold. It emerges as a personal practice of reshaping energy, using challenging experiences as a catalyst for growth. This quasi-chemical process requires us to understand the spectrum of frequencies that shape our personalities, from states of fear to elevated experiences of connection and purpose.

Our ancestral lineages carry intricate energy patterns, spiritual covenants, and practices embedded deep within our bloodlines. Celtic and African traditions, for instance, were rich with spiritual pacts that transcended individual lifetimes. These inherited influences subtly shape our experiences, often operating beyond our immediate awareness. The evidence of these patterns revealed itself in some unexpected moments during an unplanned visit to Newgrange in Ireland.

I hadn't even heard of Newgrange until the trip. But we'd snagged some ridiculously cheap flights from London and thought, "Why not?" With Scotland and Ireland in our DNA, it felt like a natural destination.

Newgrange, with its massive mounds and ancient alignments to the sun and solstices, carries a deep cosmic energy. The site is steeped in rituals and ancestral reverence – an energy hub where cosmic frequencies converge. Standing there, I was completely unprepared for what I experienced.

Upon entering the grounds, I felt an electrifying vortex, beautiful energies, and a complete sense of self-recognition. What followed was a spontaneous energy cleansing, a realignment of frequencies that left me shaken.

For days after, I felt disoriented. Something within me had shifted, and I wasn't quite sure how to process it. I shared my experience with one of the elders I met on my travels, and he listened intently before offering insight.

"You're cleansing," he said. "You walked into a space where the frequencies still align with your blueprint, your essence. This is part of the process. You just need to allow it to flow through you."

The elder further explained that the frequencies in some places match our natural frequencies like a tuning fork. That is why certain locations can trigger such intense responses. This insight made it clear to me how a location can act as a bridge between physical reality and cosmic forces, particularly for those carrying corresponding energy signatures. My body recognized something my mind couldn't explain, triggering an intense clearing process, similar to how certain frequencies can break up stagnant water.

When we talk about "cosmic alchemy," we're really discussing practical self-transformation. Instead of fighting against difficult emotions or inherited patterns, we learn to work with them. For example, turning anxiety about the future into motivation for growth or channeling anger into productive change. Aligning our understanding of our emotions to the frequencies we experience helps this alchemical process.

The universe often guides us to exactly what we need for healing, even when we don't consciously seek it. Like my spontaneous visit to Newgrange, sometimes the most powerful transformations happen when we least expect them. These moments remind us that we're active participants in our evolution, not just recipients of our fates.

Our connection to the cosmos isn't mystical or out of reach – it shows up in everyday moments of intuition, meaningful coincidences, and sudden insights. By paying attention to these experiences, we begin to understand the unique way each of us relates to the larger world around us. The cosmos is beautiful, and we should endeavor to embrace it.

THE FINAL MASK

As I've discussed, unmasking the Cosmic Mask is about dissolving the illusion of separation and realigning with the vast intelligence of the universe. When we remove this mask, we move from feeling like a passive observer of the cosmos to understanding ourselves as an active participant in its flow.

The entirety of this book is concerned with the process rather than the destination, and our journey with the cosmos is the greatest example of that idea. Through conscious exploration, we move from merely existing in the cosmos to fully embodying our role within it. The cosmos is infinite, and so the journey is everlasting.

Yet, with that in mind, where do you begin?

1. Acknowledge the Illusion of Separation

The first step in unmasking is recognizing that the mask exists in the first place – that is the same step no matter which mask you are looking to remove. So, in this instance, examine the conditioned belief we have that tells us we are isolated beings, disconnected from nature, spirit, and each other. This illusion of separateness is deeply ingrained in modern society, reinforced by an overemphasis on individualism, logic, and material reality. It disconnects us from intuition, from synchronicity, and from the knowing that we are part of something infinitely greater.

Start noticing the moments when you feel disconnected from others, from yourself, from life. Is it when you're overwhelmed? When you doubt yourself? When do you feel insignificant? These moments reveal the strength of the mask and offer clues to where healing is needed.

They signal where the mask is most potent and when you need to stop and ask yourself, "Where in my life do I feel most separate, and how would my reality shift if I viewed myself as intrinsically connected to everything around me?"

2. Tap Into Cosmic Awareness

Once you recognize the illusion, the next step is to consciously reconnect with the universe. Ancient civilizations lived in harmony with the cosmos, aligning their lives with the cycles of the stars, the moon, and the rhythms of the Earth. Modern distractions have dulled this awareness, but the ability to connect has never left us.

There is no singular, best way to tap into this awareness. Just like the journey is different for everybody, so too is the process. But here are some suggestions:

- Spend time under the open sky. Let yourself simply be with the stars, the moon, the wind, the earth. Feel their presence beyond thought.

- Meditate on the vastness of the universe. Contemplate how the elements that form your body are the same elements that make up the stars.

- Observe nature's cycles – the rising and setting of the sun, the phases of the moon, the rise and fall of the tides. Reflect on how they mirror the cycles in your own life.

- Practice breathwork. Breathe deeply, imagining yourself inhaling cosmic energy and exhaling any sense of limitation. Repeat for several minutes until you feel more expansive, open, and attuned to the present moment.

3. Reprogram Your Energy Through Healing Modalities

The Cosmic Mask is often reinforced by energy blockages – limiting beliefs, inherited trauma, and suppressed intuition. To unmask, we must clear those distortions and realign with a higher vibration.

There are several ways we can do this, but the most common practice is to actively engage in the healing modality that works for you. For example:

- **Reiki, Pranic Healing, or Quantum Healing** can help clear stagnant energy and restore flow.

- **Sound Healing:** Vibrational frequencies, such as singing bowls or tuning forks, help recalibrate your resonance with the cosmos.

- **Guided Meditation:** Visualizing cosmic light washing over you can help dissolve energy patterns that keep you feeling small or disconnected.

4. Engage in Cosmic Communication

When you begin to unmask the cosmic, you become an active participant in the universal conversation. But this is not a new conversation. The cosmos speaks to us constantly through synchronicities, dreams, intuition, and unexplainable "knowings." Learning to recognize these messages strengthens our connection.

One of the most effective things you can do as you begin to pay attention to these signposts and conversations is to keep a journal. In it, write down your questions to the universe. Try to do this before you go to bed at night, once a night, and then upon waking, write any insights, dreams, or thoughts that come up. Over time, patterns will emerge, revealing answers beyond logic.

As you begin to engage in these conversations, keep one question at the forefront of your mind: What would change if I allowed myself to fully step into cosmic connection? This is the question that can open you up and help you see these patterns that will change your life.

5. Use Cosmic Systems to Understand Your Design

Cosmic systems provide insight into your energy blueprint, revealing the natural flow of your existence. These tools don't impose limitations; they illuminate possibilities, helping you move through life with more ease and alignment.

We've already touched on Human Design, but Numerology also has its place here. Numbers carry vibrational frequencies that can provide insight into your life path, karmic lessons, and innate strengths. Your **Life Path Number** (calculated by adding the digits of your birthdate) can offer guidance on how to move in harmony with your soul's purpose.

Take the time to:

- Calculate your **Human Design Type** and reflect on how it aligns with your energy levels and interactions with others.

- Determine your **Life Path Number** and explore its meaning in relation to your journey.

6. Integrate Cosmic Awareness into Daily Life

The goal isn't to escape into cosmic consciousness but to live with one foot in the infinite and one foot firmly in the human experience. This is not an easy process, nor is it achievable overnight. Unmasking is something to be embodied daily, and with that in mind, here are some suggestions as to how you can begin that process of integration:

- **Morning Intention Setting:** Begin each day with a simple affirmation or question to align you with universal flow.

- **Mindful Presence:** Regularly pause to appreciate the beauty of life, whether in a flower, a sunset, or a moment of connection with another being.

- **Embodiment Practices:** Dance, breathe, move. Let cosmic energy flow through you.

- **Rituals for Connection:** Full moon meditations, ancestral offerings, or simple gratitude practices strengthen your bond with the unseen.

RUMINATIONS ON THE COSMOS

The Cosmic Mask convinces us that we are small, insignificant, and separate. But the truth is, we are the universe expressing itself in human form.

The process of unmasking the cosmic is not about learning something new; it's about remembering what has always been within you. In unmasking the cosmic, we strip away the illusion of separation and realign with the universal currents that have always guided you, surrendering to the vast intelligence that exists beyond human perception.

We have spent much of our lives disconnected from this truth, conditioned to believe that we are small, isolated, and bound by limitations. The cosmos does not see us this way. It knows us as we truly are – limitless, expansive, and deeply connected to the rhythm of all things. The same forces that shape the galaxies move within us. We share in universal energies and modalities. The same wisdom that governs the tides flows through our being. The mask was never real – it was only ever a veil between perception and truth.

To live unmasked is to move through the world with both feet firmly planted – one in the infinite, one in the now. It is to embrace the paradox of being both human and divine, both bound by time and yet timeless. This is not an abstract idea. It is an embodied state, a lived experience, an invitation to step into your highest expression.

The cosmos has always been speaking to you. The question is, **are you ready to listen?**

What You Have Unmasked

You've reclaimed your relationship with the unseen.
You've stepped into the frequency of wholeness,
not as an idea but as your natural state.
You've remembered that healing
doesn't just happen in the body or the mind;
it ripples through time, energy, lineage, and vibration.
You are the healer and the healed.
The student and the source.
The alchemist and the altar.
And now, the final mask has begun to fall –
not with force, but with grace.

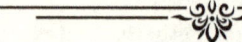

PERSONAL LIBERATION BLUEPRINT – PART V

There is a self that lives beyond the seen – beyond performance, pain, and even personality. This is your cosmic self. The part of you that remembers who you were before the world told you who to be.

But cosmic sovereignty doesn't mean bypassing reality. It means being with it fully, while still knowing you are more. This is where mystery meets integration. Where you take the abstract and root it in the everyday. This blueprint is not an escape; it's an expansion.

You are not just unmasking.

You are remembering.

Step 1: Locate Your Resistance to the Infinite

What part of you rolls its eyes at the mystical? Where does spiritual language feel too abstract or out of reach?

Purpose: Grounds you in honesty. Builds trust by acknowledging resistance before revelation.

Step 2: Name What Survival Has Taught You

What beliefs have helped you survive the tangible world – bills, betrayal, burnout – but might now be blocking your access to deeper truth?

Purpose: Honours the function of the mask while revealing its limits. You can't transcend what you haven't thanked.

Step 3: Recall a Moment You Felt Deeply Connected to Something Greater

It could be nature, music, love, grief, or silence. Describe the sensation. What did your body know before your mind could explain it?

Purpose: Makes the spiritual felt. Bridges cosmic truth to lived experience.

Step 4: Choose a Cosmic Practice

What is one small ritual – stillness, prayer, movement, creativity – that helps you return to your divine self? Commit to trying it this week, not for performance but for remembrance.

Purpose: Grounds the cosmic in the practical. Turns knowing into embodiment.

Step 5: Write a Sovereignty Statement

Complete this sentence: "Even in the chaos of the world, I remain connected to…"

Example: "…the wisdom of my soul, the rhythm of the universe, and the truth that I am more than what I can see."

Purpose: Anchors spiritual identity. You become both the seeker and the source.

PART VI
UNMASKING WHOLENESS

"The key to controlling energy
is to control the mind,
for the mind is the master of the energies."
– Swami Vivekananda

A NOTE ON WHOLENESS

There comes a moment in every person's life when something stirs inside them – an awareness, a calling, a knowing that there is more to reality than what we've been taught.

Maybe you've felt it: that invisible current running through you in moments of deep meditation, love, or grief. That undeniable presence in nature when the wind carries a whisper from something ancient. That gut feeling that speaks louder than logic.

This force – this energy – is not abstract. It is the very essence of who you are. Yet most people live disconnected from it, unaware of its power, trapped behind layers of fear, conditioning, and illusion.

The Unmasking Effect is not just about stripping away illusion. It's about reclaiming your energy, stepping into your sovereignty, and aligning with your true power.

I've traveled the world in search of this wisdom – from the hidden ethnic groups of Africa to the mystics of Asia, from the spiritual guides of South America to the Dreamtime elders of Australia. Across every culture and every practice, one universal truth remains:

We hold within us a force so powerful that it shapes reality itself.

This power is not outside of us – it has always been within.

But to access it, you must first unmask. I want to stress again that there is no single path to wholeness; there are many different ways. All you can do is get on your unique path, knowing where you are, and using the framework this book provides to achieve full wholeness.

The question is: what does wholeness actually look like when lived? How do we move from understanding this inner force to embodying it in our daily existence? The answer lies in sovereignty – the conscious integration of all aspects of ourselves into a unified expression of authentic power.

TOWARD SOVEREIGNTY

To live in wholeness is to recognize that every part of who you are – your strengths and weaknesses, light and shadow, joy and pain – has value. These facets aren't obstacles to overcome but elements to integrate. Wholeness asks us to stop running from our darkness and embrace it instead as a teacher.

At its core, wholeness unites the spiritual, emotional, and mental aspects of our being. It reconnects us with our divine essence, reminding us that we are spiritual beings having a human experience. Principles such as those in Hermetic teachings anchor us, allowing us to navigate life with clarity and intention.

Emotional intelligence is fundamental to this journey – the ability to honor and process our feelings rather than suppress them. This work involves engaging with the suppressed parts of our inner child and tending to unhealed wounds. Through this process, we develop resilience and learn to express ourselves authentically.

As a child, I struggled with the idea of a "higher self," believing the highest version of oneself was God alone. Through my journey, I discovered a deeper truth: within us lies a divine spark, a part of God that knows all and sees all. This recognition transforms our self-perception and understanding of our place in the world.

Sovereignty emerges from wholeness; they are inseparable companions on the path to self-actualization. When we achieve true integration, our mind, body, heart, and spirit work in harmony. Our values, relationships, and purpose naturally align with our inner truth, and our authentic self emerges – where both our light and shadow aspects find their rightful place in the tapestry of who we are.

But sovereignty is not built on concepts alone – it rests upon timeless principles that guide us toward authentic living.

UNMASKING ADDITIONAL UNIVERSAL TRUTHS FOR AN ALIGNED LIFE

Through my journey, I have uncovered a few universal principles that, when embraced, allow us to step into wholeness and live a life of deep alignment.

Obviously, the number one consistent truth, as mentioned in the previous chapter, is:

"We hold within us a force so powerful that it shapes reality itself."

But there is much more. To support you as you align with wholeness, here are additional truths that serve as guiding lights along the way. Awareness is important, but applying and integrating these principles is key:

1. Authenticity is Freedom

The more we unmask the false identities and societal masks, the closer we come to our true nature. Living in full authenticity is the key to inner peace and external harmony.

2. Your Energy Creates Your Reality

Thoughts, emotions, and intentions are not passive; they are active forces shaping your world. When you master your inner state, you master your external reality.

3. Fear is the Greatest Illusion

Most of what holds us back is not real – it's a construct of conditioning. When we move beyond fear, we step into infinite potential.

4. Stillness Holds the Answers

The mind seeks noise, but truth is found in silence. Whether through meditation, nature, or deep reflection, the answers we seek are always waiting in the quiet.

5. Connection is the True Currency

We are not meant to walk this path alone. Authentic relationships, built on truth and mutual growth, are among life's most powerful sources of strength and wisdom.

6. Love is the Ultimate Force

Not the romanticized version, but the raw, boundless love that connects all things. It is the essence of creation, the healer of wounds, and the most potent energy we can embody.

7. Death is an Illusion

Life is a cycle, and energy never ceases – it only transforms. When we embrace this truth, we stop living in fear of endings and start embracing the infinite nature of existence.

These seven foundational truths form the bedrock of sovereign living. They are not merely concepts to understand intellectually, but lived realities to embody daily. When we align our thoughts, actions, and energy with these principles, we begin to experience life from a place of authentic power rather than reactive survival.

FURTHER PATHS TO WHOLENESS

Beyond these foundational truths, there are even deeper principles that further support our journey to alignment:

8. Resistance is a Teacher

The things we resist most in life – our struggles, our pain, our discomfort – often hold the greatest lessons. When we lean into them instead of avoiding them, we unlock profound growth.

9. Presence is Power

Life is happening *now*. The past is memory, the future is possibility, but true power is only found in the present. When we anchor ourselves in the now, we step into our full potential.

10. Everything is a Reflection

The world around you mirrors your inner world. If there is chaos outside, there is unresolved energy within. When you change your internal state, your external reality shifts accordingly.

11. Surrender Opens the Flow

Control is an illusion. The more we cling, the more we suffer. But when we surrender – trusting in the greater flow of life – everything begins to align in ways beyond our imagination.

12. Gratitude Unlocks Abundance

What we appreciate, appreciates. Gratitude is not just an emotion; it is an energetic frequency that attracts more of what we cherish into our lives.

13. Intuition is the Truest Guide

Logic has its place, but intuition is the language of the soul. The more we listen to it, the more aligned our path becomes.

14. The Cosmos Responds to Boldness

Life rewards those who take aligned action. Fear keeps us stagnant, but courage opens doors we never knew existed. The more we trust and act upon our deeper knowledge, the more the universe conspires in our favor.

These truths are not new; they are ancient and universal. They have been whispered by sages, encoded in sacred texts, and felt in the hearts of those who have awakened.

But truth is not something to simply *know* – it is something to *become*.

To embody these principles requires more than intellectual understanding – it demands a conscious relationship with the very forces that animate existence. We must learn to work directly with energy itself.

ENERGIES AND THE INVISIBLE FORCES THAT SHAPE REALITY

Energy is the fabric of existence. It moves through everything – the air we breathe, the thoughts we think, the emotions we feel. Across civilizations, this life force has been known by many names: Chi (China), Prana (India), Ki (Japan), Ether (Africa), Ruach (Hebrew), Mana (Polynesia). It is ancient, eternal, and limitless.

And it is not separate from us. It *is* us.

Think about it:

Every thought sends shockwaves through the energy field, shaping reality.

Every emotion acts like a tuning fork, attracting experiences that match its frequency.

Every breath offers a choice to align with flow or disrupt it.

When we are in alignment, life moves effortlessly. Opportunities arise, synchronicities multiply, and creativity flows.

When we are disconnected, we experience stagnation, struggle, and chaos – both internally and externally.

The ancients understood this. They knew that by mastering energy, one could become the conscious creator of their life.

In Ghana, I met a woman who had suffered from chronic illness for years. No doctor could diagnose her condition. They told her it was "all in her head." But she *knew* something deeper was wrong.

A local healer didn't examine her body. He examined her *energy field*. What he saw was years of repressed grief, the kind that sits like a heavy stone in the heart chakra, cutting off flow, vitality, and joy.

Instead of prescribing medicine, he guided her through ritual, movement, and emotional release.

Within weeks, she began to heal.

That wasn't magic. It wasn't superstition. It was energy in motion.

The lesson?

When energy is blocked, disease manifests.

When energy flows freely, healing follows.

This is the power of unmasking – not just the illusions we wear on the outside but the invisible forces we carry within.

Understanding energy as a general principle is only the beginning. To truly master our inner state and create conscious change, we must explore the specific layers through which this energy moves – the multidimensional structure of our very being.

THE MULTIDIMENSIONAL ENERGY BODY & SELF

Most people believe they are just their physical body – a biological entity made of flesh and bones. But this is only the outermost shell of a much more complex, multidimensional energy system.

Your body is not just what you can see or touch – it is a layered structure of energies, vibration, and consciousness. Think of it like an onion – peeling back each layer reveals deeper truths about your being and provides clearer meaning to your lives.

Ancient spiritual traditions, from Hinduism and Taoism to Indigenous shamanic teachings, have long understood that humans exist beyond the physical plane. Science is now only beginning to catch up, recognizing that we are beings of frequency and vibration, interacting with an unseen field of energy, which cannot be described in normal ways.

When we understand and align these layers, we access our highest potential – mentally, emotionally, physically, and spiritually.

The 7 Layers of the Human Energy Body

1. Physical Body – The Biological Vessel Housing Your Consciousness

Your physical body is the most familiar layer, the one you see in the mirror. It is your tangible form, made of cells, organs, muscles, and bones.

But this body is not static – it is constantly renewing itself. Every seven years, nearly every cell in your body has been replaced; think about it, every seven years you're essentially a new you.

Example: When you break a bone, your body has an innate intelligence that begins healing it without your conscious effort. This intelligence flows from deeper energy layers that govern repair, growth, and regeneration.

Your physical health is, therefore, a reflection of your energy body. If your energy is misaligned, it manifests as fatigue, tension, or illness.

2. Etheric Body – The Energetic Twin of Your Physical Form

The etheric body is your energy double – an invisible structure that holds the blueprint of your physical body. It is where your chakras, meridians, and pranic energy channels reside.

This layer is why some people can feel phantom limb sensations even after an amputation – the etheric blueprint remains intact.

Example: In acupuncture and Qigong, practitioners work with the meridians – the energy pathways in the etheric body – to clear blockages and restore balance.

Energy blockages in the etheric body can lead to chronic fatigue, disease, or a sense of being "stuck" in life.

3. Astral Body – The Layer of Emotions, Dreams, and Desires

Your astral body is where all of your emotions, dreams, and desires originate. It is the realm of intuition, astral projection, and vivid dream experiences.

Have you ever woken up from a dream that felt so real it lingered throughout the day? That's because your astral body had an experience beyond the physical plane and this is very well evidenced in sleep science.

Example: Many Indigenous shamans perform soul retrieval, a practice where they journey into the astral plane to recover lost parts of a person's spirit – often fragmented due to trauma.

Emotional wounds and past experiences create imprints in the astral body, influencing how you feel, react, and attract energy into your life.

4. Mental Body – The Realm of Thoughts, Beliefs, and Inner Narratives

The mental body governs your thoughts, belief systems, and subconscious programming. It is the architect of your inner dialogue – what you tell yourself about life, relationships, and personal worth.

Example: If someone grew up hearing, "Money is hard to come by," this belief becomes embedded in their mental body, shaping their financial reality. Conversely, reprogramming the mind with affirmations like "Abundance flows easily to me" can shift energetic patterns and attract new experiences.

What you think consistently becomes the energy you project and the reality you create ...

5. Spiritual Body – The Seat of Intuition and Divine Connection

The spiritual body is the gateway to higher wisdom, where intuition, guidance, and divine inspiration flow. It is the part of you that knows you are more than this human experience.

Example: Have you ever had an inner "knowing" that defied logic? Maybe you felt drawn to a place, a book, or a person, only to realize later that it was part of a divine alignment? That was your spiritual body guiding you. For me, an example of that was my time in Newgrange. Ireland

The more you trust your inner wisdom, the stronger your spiritual connection becomes.

6. Causal Body – The Blueprint of Your Soul's Purpose

The causal body holds the memories, lessons, and experiences of your soul across lifetimes. It is where your soul contract is stored – the lessons you came here to learn and the gifts you came to share.

Example: Some people are naturally gifted in music, healing, or leadership from birth – these gifts stem from their causal body, carrying knowledge from past incarnations.

Aligning with your causal body helps you understand your purpose, your talents, and the deeper "why" behind your existence.

7. Divine Self – The Infinite, Formless Essence

At the core of it all, beyond personality and identity, is your Divine Self – pure consciousness, connected to Source, God, the Universe.

This is the eternal part of you, the observer beyond time, space, or limitation.

Example: In deep states of meditation, people experience moments of oneness, bliss, and unconditional love. They transcend their human story and remember: I AM.

When you fully embody your Divine Self, you become a conduit of love, wisdom, and limitless creation.

SUBTLE ENERGY BODIES AND CHAKRAS

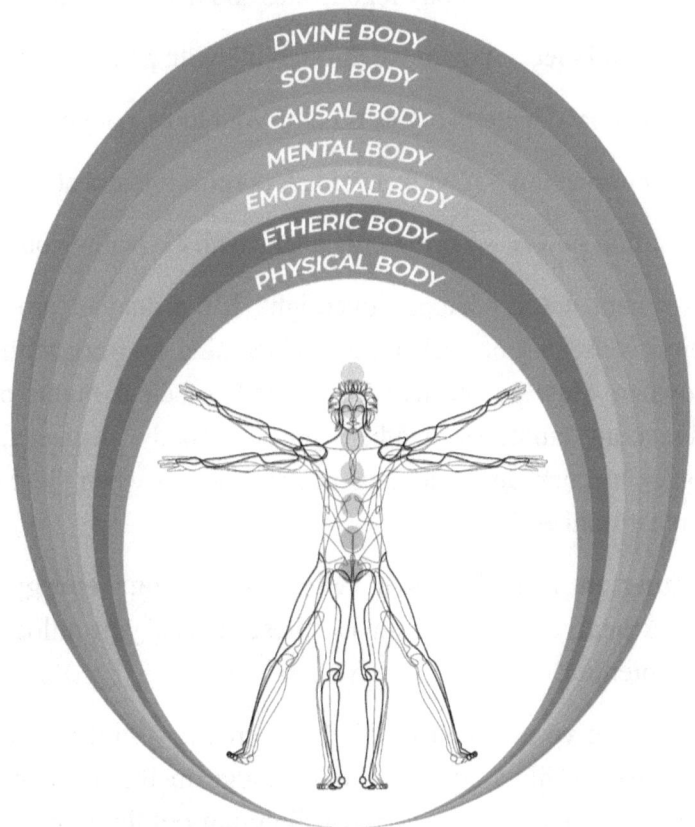

DIVINE BODY
SOUL BODY
CAUSAL BODY
MENTAL BODY
EMOTIONAL BODY
ETHERIC BODY
PHYSICAL BODY

HUMAN ENERGY BODY

"Subtle Energy Bodies" Diagram

THE TRUE POWER OF ALIGNMENT

When all layers of your being are aligned, you experience:

Physical vitality – Your body regenerates and heals naturally.

Emotional balance – You move through life with peace and clarity.

Mental mastery – Your thoughts become your tools, not your masters.

Spiritual connection – You feel guided, purposeful, and abundant.

Manifestation power – Your energy aligns with the reality you desire.

But alignment doesn't happen overnight. It's a gradual process of becoming conscious of each layer and learning to work with them intentionally. Most people live fragmented – their thoughts pulling one direction, emotions another, physical body neglected, and spiritual connection dormant. True power emerges when these layers begin to harmonize.

Everything in your life is a reflection of your energy body. When you heal, align, and unmask these layers, you unlock your highest potential.

Each mask we've explored in this book creates distortions in these energy layers. Childhood masks often lodge in the astral body as emotional patterns – the hurt child still crying out through our adult reactions. Ancestral masks influence the causal body, carrying forward unresolved experiences from generations past. Societal masks reshape the mental body, filling it with borrowed beliefs about who we should be. Cosmic masks create separation in our spiritual body, disconnecting us from our divine nature.

As we unmask, we're actually clearing these energetic imprints and restoring our natural flow. The work isn't just psychological – it's energetic. Every layer of false identity we remove allows our authentic energy to move more freely.

221

How to Strengthen and Align Your Multidimensional Energies

Physical Body → Nourish it with proper diet, exercise, rest.

- **Pay attention to:** Chronic fatigue, frequent illness, or feeling disconnected from your body.

- **Simple practice:** Daily movement that brings you joy, whether dancing, walking, or stretching.

Etheric Body → Practice breathwork, Reiki, dance, or Qigong to clear energy blockages.

- **Pay attention to:** Feeling energetically "stuck," chronic tension in specific areas, or sensitivity to others' emotions.

- **Simple practice:** 5 minutes of conscious breathing, imagining light moving through your body.

Astral Body → Keep an intuitive dream journal, explore meditation.

- **Pay attention to:** Emotional overwhelm, difficulty processing feelings, or vivid dreams that feel significant.

- **Simple practice:** Before sleep, ask for guidance through your dreams and record what you remember upon waking.

Mental Body → Reprogram limiting beliefs through affirmations and mindset work.

- **Pay attention to:** Persistent negative self-talk, repeating thought patterns, or beliefs that no longer serve you.

- **Simple practice:** Identify one limiting belief and consciously replace it with an empowering alternative throughout the day.

Spiritual Body → Trust your inner guidance, engage in prayer or silence.

- **Pay attention to:** Feeling disconnected from purpose, ignoring intuitive hits, or spiritual emptiness.

- **Simple practice:** Spend 10 minutes in silence daily, asking "What does my soul want me to know?"

Causal Body → Reflect on your life purpose, explore past-life healing.

- **Pay attention to:** Unexplained fears or talents, feeling like you don't belong in your current life, or strong reactions to certain time periods or cultures.

- **Simple practice:** Journal about your natural gifts and what themes have persisted throughout your life.

Divine Self → Surrender to the flow of life, embrace the present moment.

- **Pay attention to:** Feeling separate from life, over-identifying with your personality, or spiritual bypassing.

- **Simple practice:** Regular moments of surrendering control and trusting the larger intelligence of life.

Take a moment to sense into each layer. Where do you feel most connected? Where do you sense blockage or numbness? This awareness is your starting point for conscious alignment. Most people benefit from starting with the physical body – it's the most tangible and provides a stable foundation for working with subtle energies.

Remember: You don't need to work on all layers simultaneously. Choose one that resonates most strongly and begin there. As you align one layer, the others naturally begin to shift as well.

With this understanding of our multidimensional nature, we can now explore how these energy layers create reflections in our external reality – and how mastering this relationship becomes a key to conscious creation.

THE LAW OF MIRRORS: UNDERSTANDING YOUR INNER WORLD

"As above, so below.
As within, so without."
– The Hermetic Principle

Your external reality is more than just circumstance – it is a mirror reflecting your inner world. This universal truth, known as The Law of Mirrors, reveals how the thoughts you hold, the emotions you carry, and the shadow aspects you suppress all shape the experiences you attract.

Most people move through life reacting rather than creating, unaware that they are shaping their reality through their energy. They believe life is happening *to* them rather than *through* them. Consider how this manifests:

A chaotic mind creates a chaotic life.

A fearful heart manifests lack and obstacles.

A disciplined, focused energy draws clarity, abundance, and flow.

I once worked with a woman who found herself in a cycle of betrayal and heartbreak. She kept attracting partners who were emotionally unavailable, manipulative, or unfaithful. When we examined her inner world, we uncovered a deep-rooted belief in unworthiness, one shaped by childhood rejection.

Her external relationships mirrored her internal self-perception. As she began healing her self-worth, practicing self-love, and changing the way she spoke to herself, her outer reality shifted. She attracted a relationship that reflected her newfound confidence and wholeness.

The Inner World, A Sacred Return to Wholeness

As I mentioned in the Unmasking the Inner Child chapter of the book, I was only three years old when my mother died of cancer. Too young to understand death, but old enough to feel the sudden absence, the rupture. One day she was there, and then she wasn't. No warning, no explanation that could land in the heart of a child. Just silence, a kind of soul-void that followed me everywhere, like a shadow I didn't know I was carrying.

For years, I didn't know how deeply that loss had shaped me. I moved through life with a quiet ache, masked by smiles, achievements, and the armor I unknowingly built to protect the part of me that had been left exposed. I became a master at surviving, at being who the world wanted me to be. But deep within, my inner child had been frozen in time, waiting to be seen, to be held, to be understood.

It wasn't until I began my spiritual journey in my 30's, one marked by curiosity, desperation, and divine whispers that I started to explore my inner world. And it was within that exploration that I found him: the little boy I had abandoned. He wasn't lost. He was waiting for me...

Unmasking the Inner Child to Wholeness

As I ventured inward, I encountered memories not as events, but as energies. I didn't remember the day my mother passed, but I could feel it in my body, in the tightness in my chest, the lump in my throat, the way I recoiled from deep intimacy. These were the echoes of a child who hadn't had the words to grieve.

I began to speak to him, the inner child hiding behind the mask. I asked him what he needed. I allowed him to cry, to be angry, to feel abandoned. And I, the adult-me, stayed. That was a part of the unmasking: not in fixing, but in staying. In being the mother I never had...

225

The Unmasking Process

Grief had given me many masks! Masks of strength, independence, perfection. But each was a barrier between who I truly was and who I thought I needed to be. Unmasking wasn't just about removing layers, it was about remembering. Each time I peeled back a mask, I came closer to the truth: I am not broken. I am becoming…

This process was messy, nonlinear, often painful. But every step inward brought clarity. The inner world became a mirror, reflecting back all that had been hidden but not lost. It was there I found my soul's voice, my intuition, my divine connection. And it was in that sacred space that I began to trust again, not in the world, but in myself.

Wholeness Through Grief

Growing up, I saw my mother's death only as tragedy. But as I deepened my understanding, grief became something else entirely, it became a teacher. Her absence taught me presence. Her silence awakened my voice. Her death gave birth to my inner life.

I realized I didn't just lose my mother, I lost a sense of safety, of identity. And yet, through the grieving process, I reclaimed those things from within. I became my own safe space. I remembered that love is not lost when a person dies, or leave, it changes form. And that form can live within me, if I allow it.

Wholeness and Inner Awareness

The inner world is not some abstract spiritual concept, it is the living terrain of the soul. It holds our stories, wounds, dreams, and truths. Learning to understand this inner world, my thoughts, emotions, energy, and subconscious beliefs became the most sacred act of self-love I've ever known.

Through it, I discovered that I am more than my past. I am more than the little boy who lost his mother. I am the man who found himself. Who chose to stop running, to stop pretending, and to remember.

This is the unmasking effect and unmasking wholeness.

The sacred unveiling of the soul.

The moment you stop searching outside and come home, fully to yourself.

If you're wondering whether the inner work is worth it – **it is**.

You're not too broken, too late, or too far gone. This isn't about fixing yourself. It's about finally meeting yourself.

Your truth. Your power. Your freedom.

The life you long for begins the moment you turn inward.

So take the step.

Feel. Remember. Unmask. Heal.

You are worth the journey.

You are the journey.

> *"By not being aware of having a shadow, you declare a part of your personality to be non-existent. Then it enters the kingdom of the non-existent, which swells up and takes on enormous proportions...If you get rid of qualities you don't like by denying them, you become more and more unaware of what you are, you declare yourself more and more non-existent, and your devils will grow fatter and fatter."*
> – Carl Jung

The Shadow

Your shadow, those parts of yourself you've rejected or suppressed, acts as a powerful mirror in this process. Think of it as an energy bank. Every time you reject a part of yourself, you make a withdrawal from your power. Every time you integrate a shadow aspect, you make a massive deposit into your energy potential.

This pattern often begins in childhood:

A child scolded for expressing anger learns to repress it, their power later leaking through passive aggression and boundary struggles.

A child only loved for achievement develops perfectionism, their energy scattered through constant striving and people-pleasing.

A child taught that vulnerability is weak struggles with intimacy, their power diminished by keeping others at arm's length.

These are all extensions of what we looked at with the childhood masks. An acute example of this emerged through my work with a client who consistently found herself invisible in relationships. Partners never fully saw her, friends overlooked her, bosses ignored her contributions.

Through shadow integration, she discovered the truth: She was the first to disappear. She leaked power by downplaying her needs, suppressing her emotions, and making herself small to avoid rejection. When she began reclaiming her power – letting herself be seen without self-censorship – the external world began mirroring her wholeness instead of her invisibility.

Embracing the Shadow and The Light I Found in the Dark

I used to believe the path to unmasking was about becoming more light – more love, more joy, more peace. But I've come to understand that deep unmasking requires something more: the courage to walk into the dark. Into the parts of myself I had hidden, denied, or forgotten. Into the shadow.

My shadow journey began with my inner child, the tender part of me left shattered when my mother died as we discussed earlier.

I learned to survive by masking my pain, becoming who I thought I needed to be… pleasing, achieving, strong. But underneath the mask was a child still frozen in time, waiting for someone – *me* – to come back for him.

As I turned inward, I found him. Not in memory, but in feeling – in the tightness in my chest, the avoidance of intimacy, the constant striving to be enough. These weren't just habits. I realized the shadow wasn't some evil lurking within me. It was a wounded part of me, still trying to protect me.

I began to unmask, not to shame these parts, but to understand them. To hold space for the scared child, to offer him the love he never received. That was the beginning of my true unmasking: not escaping the past, but re-entering it with compassion and presence.

As I unmasked, I began to see a bigger picture. My personal shadows were deeply intertwined with the shadows of the world around me. I was conditioned not only by my own masks but by a culture that values performance over presence, strength over softness, and control over feeling.

I saw how society teaches us to wear masks to hide our grief, to suppress our truth, to fit into systems that don't serve our souls. And I saw how much of my suffering came from internalizing these societal shadows. Unmasking meant reclaiming my voice, my softness, my right to exist beyond roles or expectations.

In facing the societal shadow, I wasn't just healing myself, I was reclaiming my humanity.

And then there were the shadows that weren't even mine. As I dug deeper, I felt the weight of unspoken grief, generational silence, and inherited beliefs passed down through my lineage.

I could feel the residue of unresolved pain, the coping mechanisms etched into my DNA.

These were ancestral shadows, echoes from those who came before me. I began to realize that some of my fears, my patterns, my emotional responses weren't born from my life alone. They were legacies... And I had a choice: to repeat them or to unmask and heal them.

By confronting these inherited wounds, I became a living altar where the generations before me could find peace. I did and continue to do the work they couldn't. And in doing so, I offered freedom to those who will come after me.

On a soul level, I began to understand that the shadow exists not just in people or systems, but in the very fabric of creation. The darkness is not something to fear. It is the womb of transformation. The mystery from which all life emerges.

The cosmic shadow taught me to embrace paradox, that light and dark are not enemies, but dance partners. That unmasking is not about perfection, but wholeness. And that what I once ran from was never meant to destroy me, it was meant to awaken me.

This is the unmasking effect: The sacred unveiling of the soul. The reclaiming of what was hidden, the integration of what was lost.

Through the shadow, I didn't just heal. I remembered. Who I was. Who I am. Who I've always been beneath the masks.

Emotional Alchemy and Converting Pain to Power

Consider the man I met during a retreat. He had spent years drowning his emotions in work, distractions, and external validation. When his marriage ended, he could no longer outrun the pain. His energy was scattered across countless distractions, leaving him depleted and disconnected.

Through shadow work, he sat with the emotions he had spent years avoiding. He discovered his greatest fear, being unlovable, was an old wound, a childhood pattern that had shaped his adult relationships. The moment he allowed himself to fully feel his grief, his energy transformed. He no longer needed to prove his worth to others; he reclaimed it from within.

These stories illustrate the life-changing power of mirror work, but understanding the principle is only the beginning. To truly master this dynamic, and to become conscious creators rather than unconscious reactors, we need practical tools for integration.

Download The Complimentary Unmasking Effect Shadow Work Journal from www.UnmaskingResources.com:

MASTERING YOUR INNER MIRRORS AND SHADOWS

To truly unmask the inner Mirrors and integrate your shadow, start with these transformative practices:

1. Self-Reflection and Pattern Recognition

Begin by observing the recurring patterns in your life. Notice the situations, relationships, or challenges that keep reappearing. These patterns offer a glimpse into the beliefs and energies you're holding within.

2. Energy Command Reprogramming

Shift your inner dialogue from limiting thoughts like:

> "I'm not good enough.
>
> Love is conditional.
>
> I always mess things up."

Instead, reframe these beliefs in empowering terms:

> "I am inherently worthy.
>
> I am worth loving.
>
> I release what no longer serves me."

3. Emotional Mastery

Rather than letting your emotions control your actions, pause and observe them.

Transform your emotions from energy leaks into powerful forces that propel you forward.

Ask yourself, "What is this emotion here to teach me?"

4. Vibration Elevation

Foster positive emotions like gratitude, joy, and love. These high-frequency states don't just feel good; they accelerate positive change. Don't wait for external circumstances to change; embody these elevated emotions now.

The results of this inner work will be substantive:

- **Deeper Self-Love and Acceptance** – No longer scattered by internal conflict

- **Emotional Liberation and Peace** – Transforming emotions from drains into sources of power

- **Freedom from Repetitive Cycles** – Breaking free from old patterns that no longer serve you

- **Authentic Relationships Based on Truth** – Power returned from the grip of self-abandonment

Remember, you are not a passive participant in life. You are its creator. Reality doesn't simply happen to you; it responds to you. Your shadow doesn't diminish your power; it completes you. Every aspect you integrate becomes another source of creative force.

Let's move on to take a deeper look at the boundless power of the mind as we continue to unmask.

THE LIMITLESS POWER OF THE MIND

Your mind is more than just a thinking tool; it is the architect of your reality, the command center of your energy. Every thought, belief, and intention you hold sends ripples through the energy field, shaping your experiences.

"Energy follows intention, and
intention is born in the mind."

Think of your mind as a sculptor. Every thought carves out your future. Some people sculpt with precision, shaping lives filled with success, health, and love. Others, unaware of their power, let chaotic thoughts chip away at their potential, leaving behind uncertainty and stagnation.

Imagine two people standing at the edge of a river.

- One has a clear goal – they want to cross to the other side. Their mind is focused, so they find the right tools, build a bridge, and confidently step forward.

- The other person hesitates. They want to cross but doubt their ability. They take a step forward, then back, looking for another route but second-guessing every choice. Their scattered energy prevents movement.

That is how the mind works. When it is disciplined, clear, and focused, it acts like a magnet for manifestation. When it is scattered and chaotic, it leaks energy, weakening your ability to create.

Here is another example to consider

- A flashlight spreads light in all directions – it illuminates but lacks intensity.

- A laser beam concentrates all its energy into a single, powerful point.

Your mind works the same way. If your thoughts are scattered, jumping from worry to doubt, from past regret to future fear, your energy disperses like a weak flashlight. But when your mind is focused and disciplined, you harness laser-like energy, cutting through obstacles and manifesting your desires.

I once met a man in Bali who spent years dreaming of opening a healing retreat, but his mind was filled with doubt.

He thought, "What if I fail? What if people don't come? Maybe I should try something else first?"

Each thought leaked energy; he was pouring his focus into fears instead of his vision. When he trained his mind through meditation, visualization, and daily affirmations, his energy aligned with his goal. Within a short time, the retreat center became a reality.

This principle of mental mastery isn't limited to entrepreneurs or dreamers – it applies to every aspect of life, including our most fundamental beliefs about abundance and possibility. Sometimes the most profound transformations happen when we reprogram our deepest conditioning about what's available to us.

THE MAN WHO REPROGRAMMED HIS REALITY

I remember another example of the power of the mind...

I met him on a humid afternoon in Kingston, Jamaica. He was a man with calloused hands and a tired spirit, burdened by years of struggle. His days were filled with relentless effort, laboring in the sun, chasing opportunities that always seemed just out of reach. No matter how hard he worked, financial security remained a distant dream, like a mirage in the desert.

As we spoke, I noticed something deeper than his external hardship. His energy was speaking through his words, revealing the unseen forces shaping his reality.

"Money is hard to come by. I always fall short. I can never get ahead."

It wasn't just language; it was a program running his life, a deeply embedded energy script dictating his outcomes before he even took action. His struggles weren't just financial; they were vibrational.

I asked him to sit with me. We began with meditation, which was simply sitting still for a few seconds… helping him step beyond his habitual thoughts and into the present moment where transformation becomes possible. Before we could tune the frequency, we had to clear the static.

Through simply being present and breathing intentionally, he started releasing years of tension. Through visualization, he no longer saw himself as a man chasing money but as a magnet for abundance. We worked on reprogramming his internal dialogue, replacing scarcity-driven thoughts with affirmations of prosperity:

"I am a magnet for abundance. Wealth flows to me effortlessly. I am worthy of financial freedom. I am financial freedom!

At first, the words felt foreign to him. Years of hardship had conditioned him to believe that life was a battle. But slowly, his energy began to shift. He started embodying the creator of his reality instead of the victim of his circumstances.

Within a year, his financial situation transformed, not through blind luck but through energy alignment and having a daily practice. He attracted new opportunities, unexpected sources of income, and a business connection that elevated his career. His internal world had changed, and the external world responded accordingly.

This story isn't unique to him. How many of us are running subconscious programs of limitation? How often do we unknowingly send out energy commands that reinforce our struggles?

The transformation this man experienced didn't happen through willpower alone – it required specific tools and practices that anyone can learn. The mind, like any instrument, can be tuned to operate at its highest frequency.

RE-TUNING OUR MINDS

The mind is like a radio – it can be tuned to different frequencies. Most people unknowingly operate on stations filled with static: worry, doubt, limitation, and fear. But just as you can turn the dial to find a clearer signal, you can retune your mental frequency to align with abundance, clarity, and possibility.

The man in Jamaica didn't just change his thoughts – he changed his entire mental operating system. This kind of transformation requires specific practices that gradually shift your default frequency from scarcity to abundance, from fear to trust.

Your energy is your blueprint. If you shift the frequency, you shift your life. Here are a few additional ways to align:

1. **Meditation/Intentional Breathing** – Enter the sacred space of stillness where thoughts dissolve into pure awareness. Here, in the gap between mental chatter, you discover the infinite well of consciousness that exists beyond the thinking mind. This practice builds the foundation for all energy mastery.

2. **Visualization** – Your mind doesn't distinguish between vividly imagined experiences and physical reality. When you paint detailed mental pictures of your desired state, you're literally rewiring your neural pathways and energy field to align with that vision. Let your imagination become the blueprint for manifesting your goals.

3. **Affirmations** – Words carry vibrational frequencies that ripple through your entire being. Choose declarations that resonate with your soul's truth, not just your ego's desires. Speak them with full emotional engagement, allowing each statement to penetrate deeply into your subconscious landscape.

4. **Journaling** – The written word acts as a bridge between your conscious and unconscious realms. As you write your thoughts on the pages, hidden wisdom surfaces, revealing the subtle ways your energy either flows or becomes blocked. Let your journal become a text of self-discovery.

Your consciousness shapes every particle of your reality. Master these tools not to control life, but to dance with it more skillfully. As your mind learns to direct energy with precision and grace, you naturally step into alignment with your highest potential.

Yet the mind, powerful as it is, does not exist in isolation. It operates through a physical vessel that must be honored and cared for. True mastery requires the integration of mental clarity with physical vitality.

WHOLENESS AND THE BODY

Having considered the importance of the mind, let us now move on to similarly consider another key aspect of the human experience: the body.

Your body is more than a vessel; it is the foundation of your experience and the bridge between the physical world and energy. Yet, many of us move through life disconnected from it, pushing past discomfort, numbing pain, or ignoring signals until illness or exhaustion forces us to pay attention.

Every thought and emotion leaves an imprint on the body. Stress manifests as tightness in the shoulders, fear knots the stomach, and unprocessed grief lingers as fatigue or tension. The body is constantly communicating, storing experiences in muscles, fascia, and the nervous system. When we ignore these messages, energy stagnates, leading to imbalances that affect both physical health and spiritual alignment.

To sustain higher states of awareness, the body must be strong and balanced. Movement, breathwork, proper nutrition, and rest are not just wellness practices – they are the foundation of energy integrity.

When we take care of our bodies, we create the capacity to hold more energy, process emotions effectively, and stay grounded in the present. Rather than something to transcend, the body is something to fully inhabit. The more connected you are to it, the more fully you step into your power.

When mind and body work in harmony, this integration naturally extends into every area of life, including how we create and relate to abundance. True sovereignty isn't just internal; it manifests in our external choices and circumstances.

FINANCIAL SOVEREIGNTY

Living in this authentic state of wholeness also extends to our financial choices. True financial liberation isn't just about making money; it's about aligning the way we create wealth with our values, purpose, and impact. It's the difference between working to survive and allowing income to flow as an expression of who we are.

When we operate from a place of wholeness, our financial decisions shift. Work stops feeling like a constant grind and instead becomes a channel for authentic creation. Rather than chasing success by external standards, we find ways to generate income that nourishes both our spirit and our material well-being.

I learned this firsthand when I built my marketing agency from the ground up. On the surface, I had achieved financial success – clients, revenue, and all the metrics of a thriving business. But something felt deeply off. Many of the industries I worked with didn't align with me energetically anymore.

The turning point came during a client meeting. We had just finished discussing record-breaking ROI, yet the moment I logged off the call, I felt sick. Literally. I went to the bathroom and threw up. It was my body's way of telling me something wasn't right. The money was there, but the alignment was missing. I couldn't ignore it any longer.

So I made a choice. I sold a large portion of my business and redirected my focus. I began investing in industries and projects that resonated with me, focusing on businesses with a conscience and creating financial structures that supported my family while staying true to my energy.

When your work aligns with your truth, success takes on a different meaning. It's no longer about relentless hustle; it's about flow. The energy you invest comes back in ways that support both your well-being and the world around you.

That doesn't mean bypassing responsibility. As my grandmother used to say, "You still have to chop wood and carry water." But when you're aligned, even the necessary tasks of life take on meaning. You handle them with efficiency, intention, and a sense of purpose.

Financial sovereignty isn't about escaping the system; it's about creating a system that works for you. It's about understanding that wealth is an extension of your energy and that when you act from a place of wholeness, abundance becomes a natural byproduct.

This same principle of alignment extends beyond money into the realm of human connection. When we no longer need to perform for survival, our relationships transform from transactions into authentic exchanges of energy and truth.

UNMIRRORED RELATIONSHIPS

Just as wholeness transforms the way we approach work and money, it also reshapes the way we connect with others. Relationships built on alignment don't require force; they unfold naturally, rooted in authenticity and truth.

When you embody wholeness, your presence shifts. You no longer need to chase, convince, or control. Instead, you radiate a frequency that draws the right people toward you and allows others to drift away without resistance. You aren't striving to be understood; you're simply living in a way that speaks for itself.

1. Closest Relationships (Friends & Family)

Wholeness allows you to show up fully for the people who matter most. When you're grounded in your truth, your relationships deepen, not because you're trying to fix or change anyone but because you're offering your presence from a space of love and acceptance.

But this also means some relationships will shift. As you grow, certain connections may no longer align. It isn't about cutting people off; it's about recognizing when a relationship has served its purpose and allowing it to evolve naturally.

For example, I recently reconnected with a childhood friend I'd known since I was two years old. We grew up in Jamaica, inseparable as kids. But as we sat together after years apart, I realized we had become very different people. There was no animosity, just a quiet recognition that the bond we once shared had changed. And that was okay. I didn't force the connection or walk away with judgment; I simply held space for what had been, with gratitude.

2. Regular Interactions (Colleagues, Acquaintances)

When you're whole within yourself, your everyday interactions become effortless. You no longer shrink yourself to fit in or seek approval from others. Instead, you move through the world with clarity and integrity, bringing your full self into every exchange.

This doesn't mean you'll always be understood. Some people may misinterpret your authenticity as indifference or arrogance. But that's not your burden to carry. When you stop seeking validation, you give yourself permission to simply be.

3. Strangers & the Wider World

Wholeness extends even to those you don't know personally. It shifts the way you engage with the world, not from a place of separateness but from a deeper sense of connection. You begin to see people as reflections of the same universal energy, not as "others."

This openness allows you to give freely, not just materially, but with your energy. A kind word, a moment of presence, an act of service … These small gestures carry immense power when they come from a space of wholeness.

Let me be real: the process isn't always easy. Growth can feel isolating at times. As you unmask old conditioning, some relationships will naturally fade. But that isn't loss; it's alignment. The right people will find you when you're vibrating at your highest truth.

When conflict arises, your foundation remains steady. You don't overly react to wounds; you instead respond with wisdom. You've done the inner work. You've learned to navigate challenges with clarity and grace.

At its core, wholeness in relationships is about being present, being real, and letting go of control. It's trusting that those who are meant to walk beside you will do so because your paths are meant to align, not because you've held onto them.

But what does this authentic presence actually look like in daily life? How do we navigate the gap between understanding these principles and embodying them in our moment-to-moment choices? Sometimes the most profound shifts happen through the smallest acts of self-honoring.

THE UNMASKED SELF

I want to share a personal anecdote – a seemingly simple one, but it was very impactful for me. Growing up, I was always neat and polished. My school uniform was immaculately pressed, with a sharp seam down the back, and my hair was trimmed weekly or every other week. The conditioning around appearances was clear: clean-cut was good, and long hair was bad. Even the idea of growing "locks" was looked down upon; the word "dread" in "dreadlocks" itself implied something negative.

At some point, I decided I didn't want to keep cutting my hair or shaving – not because I had anything against it, but simply because I no longer felt like doing it. I wanted to explore how it felt to let go of this ingrained expectation. After a few months of not cutting my hair, people started asking questions. Friends, family, even strangers – everyone seemed puzzled. They all commented that it didn't look good, that it was unkempt. The more questions I got, the more I realized how much of a persona I'd built around my appearance.

This experience made me uncomfortable at first. I wasn't just stepping outside of *societal* expectations; I was stepping outside of my *own*. But as time went on, I grew comfortable in my unshaven, unkempt appearance. I started to see the layers of conditioning that had dictated how I presented myself for years, and I felt the courage to let them go.

When I finally decided to cut my hair again, it wasn't out of obligation or pressure; it was because I wanted to. I did it on my own terms, as an act of sovereignty. That choice, seemingly small on the surface, was a profound act of reclaiming my authenticity.

That is what living authentically means: not being bound by conditioning but making choices from a place of alignment with who you truly are. It's a constant process of questioning, shedding, and owning your truth, even when it feels uncomfortable or goes against the grain.

Here are a few questions for you to consider:

1. What aspects of my identity have been shaped by societal conditioning rather than my true self?

Reflect on the beliefs, habits, and expectations you've inherited. Which ones genuinely align with you, and which ones feel like they were imposed by external influences?

2. Where in my life am I making choices out of obligation rather than personal truth?

Consider the decisions you make daily – big and small. Are they rooted in authenticity, or are they driven by fear, expectation, or the desire to conform?

3. What would it feel like to release one external expectation and embrace my true self fully?

Imagine shedding one layer of conditioning – whether in appearance, career, relationships, or self-expression. How would it feel to move through the world freely, without that imposed limitation?

The hair story may seem trivial, but it represents something significant: the courage to make choices from the inside out. Every time we choose authenticity over approval, we reclaim a piece of our power. These small acts of sovereignty accumulate, creating a life that truly belongs to us.

WHOLENESS

Wholeness is not a destination. It is a continual process of integration, a conscious unfolding of all that we are. It is the reclamation of the scattered parts of ourselves, the weaving together of light and shadow, strength and vulnerability, mind and body, spirit and form.

This journey is not about perfection or achieving some enlightened state. It is about presence, about meeting ourselves fully in every moment, without resistance or avoidance. It is about embracing the contradictions within us and seeing them not as flaws but as the necessary dualities that shape our existence.

We have been taught to compartmentalize, to see our emotions, our physical selves, our relationships, and our purpose as separate entities, disconnected from one another. But wholeness asks us to break down these artificial barriers. It reminds us that our financial choices, the way we love, the way we work, and the way we treat our bodies all are an expression of the same energy. When we move in alignment, every part of our existence begins to harmonize.

Yet, this path is not without its challenges. To embrace wholeness, we must confront the parts of ourselves we've long ignored. We must acknowledge the ways we have suppressed our emotions, outsourced our power, and lived according to expectations that were never truly our own. There is discomfort in this process – a shedding of old layers, a recalibration of what it means to be authentic.

The beauty of wholeness is that it does not demand rigidity. It is not about constructing a fixed identity but about allowing ourselves the freedom to evolve. Just as we are not meant to remain stagnant in our beliefs, we are not meant to be bound by past versions of ourselves. **Wholeness grants us permission to shift, to realign, to continuously refine the way we move through the world.**

Ultimately, to live in wholeness is to live in sovereignty: to make choices that honor our deepest truth rather than reacting from conditioning or fear. It is to recognize that we are the creators of our reality, shaping our experiences through our thoughts, our energy, and our presence.

There is no final step, no finish line. Only the ongoing invitation to step more fully into ourselves, to claim the power that has always been ours, and to walk forward in the knowledge that we have always been whole.

UNMASKED

As we reach the end of this journey, it's clear that unmasking is not an act of destruction but one of liberation. We began by exploring the masks we inherit, those shaped by history, family, and society. Along the way, we discovered that those masks were never truly ours; they were tools of survival, stories passed down, and layers meant to shield us from pain. But in uncovering them, we did not erase the past; we reclaimed it.

Throughout this book, we have traveled through ancestral lineage, childhood wounds, societal expectations, and even cosmic influence. Each step revealed a truth often hidden: that our stories, though shaped by the past, are ultimately ours to rewrite.

We are not bound by inherited pain or predefined roles. We are not confined to the survival strategies of those who came before us. Instead, we stand at the intersection of history and possibility, holding the power to transform not only our lives but also the legacy we pass forward.

Through my travels across over 100 countries, I witnessed firsthand the universal nature of these struggles. In Ghana, I stood in the dungeons where my ancestors once suffered, feeling the weight of their unspoken stories. In Australia, I learned of indigenous traditions that preserved wisdom despite centuries of oppression.

On sacred lands in South America, I engaged in rituals that illuminated the unseen threads connecting past, present, and future.

Each place, each experience, deepened my understanding that the journey of unmasking is not confined to one culture or one life. It is a calling that spans generations and geographies.

Unmasking is a continuous process, one that demands courage, self-awareness, and a willingness to embrace both our light and our shadow. There is no final destination, no perfect state of being in which we are wholly free of masks. Instead, there is the ongoing practice of presence: the choice, in each moment, to live in alignment with our truth.

To unmask is to reclaim our power. It is to honor our ancestors by evolving beyond their struggles. It is to acknowledge pain without allowing it to define us. It is to break cycles through integration, through understanding what has shaped us while choosing what will sustain us, not through rejection of that history.

As you close this book, know that the journey does not end here; it has only just begun. The work of unmasking continues in the choices you make, in the stories you tell yourself, and in the authenticity with which you move through the world. With each step forward, you are not only uncovering yourself, you are setting a new path for those who will follow.

You are unmasked. You are free.

A FINAL WORD FROM ME

What does it mean to become whole?

What does it look like to finally take off the mask you were handed, the one shaped by survival, by expectation, by fear, and put on the one you chose?

For me, the old mask looked like hustle. Achievement. Hyper-structure. 80-hour weeks, which I used to think I wore like a badge of honour. That mask gave me certainty – but it also gave me distance. From myself, from joy, from being truly presence.

I thought wholeness was just about healing. In time, I've learned it's also about remembering.

It's remembering that two things can be true, that you can be strong and still scared. That you can be shedding and still sovereign. That the old mask may try to return... but you don't have to let it lead you.

For me, this realization has happened very personally and very recently. While writing this book, the mask tried to come back. It tried to come back many times. The voice would tell me:

"Who are you to write this?"

"What if no one cares?"

"Play small. Stay safe. Be quiet."

But I didn't listen. Instead, I chose to feel it all, the doubt, the grief, the resistance, and then write anyway. In doing so, I came into contact with a deeper truth:

Wholeness isn't about being finished. It's about being real. It's not about never wearing a mask again; it's about knowing when you are and why … and choosing differently. It's also about knowing that the masks will challenge you again in the future but that you will overcome these challenges. The masks that may have subsumed you before simply cause doubts.

What happens when you address these challenges?

You don't just set yourself free ... You offer that **freedom to others.**

Because, in the end, this is not just a personal journey. It's a collective remembering:

Of who we are beneath performance. Of what we carry in our bones, our blood, our frequency. Of the truth that authenticity isn't just a lifestyle – it's an offering.

So, if you've read these pages and something in you shifted, even if we never speak, even if you never reach out, know this:

You are already whole.

You were never broken.

You are not behind.

You are more than enough.

And from someone who knows what it's like to feel unworthy of their own voice, I want to say:

I know you are amazing. I hope you know that too.

NEXT STEPS

The journey of unmasking continues beyond these pages. If you're feeling called to go deeper into this work, I invite you to join me in one of the following ways:

At the www.UnmaskingEffect.com you can learn more about my work, practice, and can interact with me directly through my 1:1 Ascension Coaching.

For insights and conversations about unmasking, sovereignty, and authentic living, tune into The Unmasking Effect Podcast. It is available on Spotify; search for The Unmasking EffectTM: Reinventing Your Reality Podcast by Ike Anderson or you can scan the QR code.

If you feel drawn to learn more about the ancestral healing journey, visit www.ExploringLegacy.org to learn about our work in West

Africa. Through the Exploring Legacy Foundation, my wife and family seek to provide life-changing experiences for young adults of African ancestry. We aim to help young adults connect with their roots, especially through our African Birthright & Rite of Passage Program.

If you've enjoyed *The Unmasking Effect* and would like to engage with similarly-minded people, you will find an amazing community here.

Each step you take toward authenticity creates imprints that extend far beyond your own life. You've already begun the journey – now let's continue it together.

ABOUT THE AUTHOR

Ike Anderson is a transformational guide, entrepreneur, and spiritual seeker who has dedicated his life to personal growth and helping others unmask their authentic selves. With over 25 years of experience in the digital marketing and entrepreneurial space, Ike transitioned from serving attorney clients with limited purpose alignment to focusing on purpose-driven work that resonates deeply with his values. His journey spans over 100 countries, with profound spiritual experiences across continents, and he now channels that wisdom into helping others unlock their full potential.

Ike's life took a transformative turn when he and his family embarked on a five-year world-wide journey retracing their ancestral paths. This experience catalyzed deep personal healing, leading him to explore spiritual traditions, ancestral wisdom, and the complexities of human identity. Along the way, he gained invaluable insights into human design and personal transformation, blending this knowledge with his entrepreneurial experience.

Through personal experiences of loss, including the early death of his mother, and life-changing moments like visiting slave dungeons in Ghana, Ike developed a compassionate approach to healing. He helps individuals confront and release societal and personal conditioning, guiding them toward a path of authenticity.

A father of three and a lifelong student of spirituality, and personal growth, Ike believes true transformation comes from understanding inherited patterns and consciously choosing a path of healing. Now, he coaches a select group of clients, offering strategic insights and support to help them grow their businesses while aligning with their purpose. His work is grounded in the belief that when we connect deeply with our purpose and heritage, we unlock the potential for both personal and professional success.

Ike's philosophy centers on the idea that living authentically requires the courage to release the masks we wear and embrace who we truly are. He looks forward to exploring potential collaborations that align with his values and purpose-driven mission.

Ike and his wife run the Exploring Legacy Foundation, which helps young adults 18-25 years old explore their lineage through experiential and spiritual journeys, including sacred ancestral healing, to connect with their culture and heritage.

RESOURCES, GUIDES AND MATERIALS

To support your journey with this book, download the **Unmasking Effect Worksheets** – designed to accompany and deepen your experience.

Visit: www.UnmaskingResources.com

These tools are here to help you reflect, integrate, and embody the wisdom within these pages.

DID YOU LOVE THIS BOOK?

*****

I'd be honored if you'd share your thoughts

by leaving an honest review on Amazon!

www.ingramcontent.com/pod-product-compliance
Lightning Source LLC
Chambersburg PA
CBHW021220130626
46554CB00004B/1290